My Best Recipe

Winning Recipes
from
The Honolulu Advertiser

Bess Press
P.O. Box 22388
Honolulu, HI 96823

Cover design: Marcie Farias

Graphics: Rick Padden

My Best Recipe: Winning Recipes from The Honolulu Advertiser
Honolulu, Hawaii: Bess Press, Inc.
144 pages

ISBN: 0-935848-96-7

Printed in Hong Kong

Table of Contents

Chicken

Seafood

Vegetarian or Combination

Desserts

Breads, Cakes, & Cookies

Pastries, Pies, Puddings, and Tortes

Introduction

It all started in March of 1990. Spring was upon us and it seemed like the perfect time to kick off a recipe contest in *The Honolulu Advertiser* Food Section.

We decided to call it the "My Best Recipe Contest and invite our readers who enjoy cooking to share their favorite recipes. No doubt it's every host or hostess' dream to have a file of menus that never fail--one that he or she can rely on for all occasions, whether formal or informal.

Readers were asked to submit recipes in three categories: appetizer, entrée, or dessert. Each week we selected an outstanding recipe and shared it with our readers in the Wednesday Food Section. The three top winners in the three categories were selected in November, and each received a $100 cash prize.

The contest was a success from the beginning because Islanders not only enjoy good food, but they're also innovative, borrowing flavors and culinary styles from the East and West. And they know how to enhance their creations with fresh produce and seafood abundant in Hawai`i.

All the recipes submitted are family favorites, some were acquired during travels to exotic places, others were passed down from one generation to another, and many are the cooks' originals.

From the beginning the response was overwhelming, with mail coming from all over the state. Even tourists sent in recipes before their departures, or mailed them in once they'd returned home.

By the time the contest ended in November 1990, there were countless calls and letters requesting that we continue the column. So by popular demand the second "My Best Recipe" Contest was begun in January 1991.

The response has been even greater the second time around, with readers suggesting that the best recipes be compiled into book form.

So, here it is: the "My Best Recipe" cookbook. Included are recipes that appeared in the Food Section during 1990 and 1991. Since our second annual contest ran through October 1991, and this book went to press in August 1991, not all the 1991 winning recipes are included.

Mahalo to those who've shared their treasured recipes so others can enjoy them. From this kitchen camaraderie has come a collection of best recipes for Island cooks to treasure.

Patsy Matsuura,

Food Editor

Appetizers

Cassandra Aoki's Vietnamese Spring Rolls can be made ahead.

Most busy people prefer simple recipes that can be prepared in a jiffy, but not **Cassandra Aoki**. She enjoys fancy cooking even after a hard day at the office. A secretary at the University of Hawaii School of Nursing, Aoki found this recipe in an Asian cookbook at the library and has been making it for the last few years. The recipe called for diced pork cutlet, but Aoki changed it to ground pork and switched from

1 can of crab meat to imitation crab meat and used more long rice. She also experimented with the lemon grass condiment instead of using fresh lemon grass.

Aoki said she attempted to capture the taste and smell of the spring rolls and dipping sauce prepared locally in the Thai or Vietnamese restaurants. She has received many compliments on these spring rolls.

Vietnamese Spring Rolls

1-1/2 cups chopped long rice (soak 10 minutes and drain)
6 green onions, chopped fine
1 pound ground pork
3 or 4 sticks of mock crab, chopped
2 tablespoons fish sauce from Thailand (at Asian Market or supermarkets)
1/4 teaspoon ground black pepper
1/2 to 1 teaspoon dried lemon grass (available as condiment at Asian Market)
1 package lumpia wrappers or dried rice paper rounds (small size)

Condiments:
About 3 small lettuce (Manoa is best)
Fresh mint (optional)
1 hothouse cucumber, cut into 2-inch strips

Sauce:
1/4 cup sugar
1/2 cup water
1/2 cup vinegar
1 tablespoon fish sauce
1 chili pepper, crushed
1 tablespoon grated or shredded carrot

Soak long rice in hot water. Drain, chop and mix with rest of ingredients in order in large bowl. Blend with hand to make sure pork is not too lumpy and mixes with crab.

Use regular spring roll/lumpia wrapper (in frozen section of market) or if you want see-through crisp rolls, buy dried wrappers at the Asian Market or in Chinatown. When using dried ones, work next to sink with warm water running slightly. Wet both sides quickly and lay on plate to fill and roll. Use about 2 tablespoons of filling for 12-inch rolled size. Fold in at sides and roll away from you. Place on seam on wax paper-lined cookie sheet to freeze. Then pull off wax paper and put in rolls in large freezer bag.

The rolls may be fried until golden brown and crisp on medium heat in about 1/4 cup of oil or steamed for 5 to 7 minutes. Mix sauce (double for more than 2 people) in order of ingredients when ready to serve. Put in saimin-size bowls for easier dipping.

Wrap each spring roll with a cucumber strip in lettuce and dip in sauce. Mint is used separately. Makes 21 to 24 2-inch size rolls or 40 1-1/2-inch size rolls.

Making the rolls seems like lots of work, but it's not if you prepare them ahead and freeze them. They're great for weekend company or for a quick weekday dinner.

3

Kitty Gharda's Pupu Pakora is similar to tempura but has a subtle, distinctively Indian spicing.

"My Best Recipe" judges commented favorably on **Kitty Gharda's Pupu Pakora** batter, especially its crispness. Because of the baking powder, the batter coating is always light.

Gharda is originally from Eastern Canada. A freelance writer, she met her husband, Dinshaw, in Berkeley, California, where they were married. Gharda learned to make Pupu Pakora from her sister-in-law on her first trip to India with her Bombay-born husband. Dinshaw and Gharda make them together, and their only break with tradition is that they both prefer the ones made with mushrooms.

Gharda is interested in Indian cooking, and tries to serve healthy dishes. Because she lives in a condominium and is unable to plant vegetables in the backyard, she grows lemon grass and basil in a rooftop garden.

4

Pupu Pakora

Mushrooms, zucchini, green
 pepper, eggplant, sweet potatoes
 or bananas

Batter:
1 cup flour
1-1/2 teaspoons salt
1/4 teaspoon red chili powder
1/3 teaspoon turmeric
1 tablespoon oregano (optional)
1/4 teaspoon cumin
1/2 tablespoon coriander (optional)
1-1/2 tablespoons lemon juice
1/3 teaspoon baking powder
Enough water to make batter like
 pancake batter

Stir dry ingredients together. Add
lemon juice and water, and stir until
smooth. Dip vegetables in batter
and deep-fry in hot oil. Drain on
paper towels before serving.

Pakora can be served with a dip
or a chutney.

---

*Pupu Pakora goes especially well with
chutneys made with mint or Chinese
parsley. An addicting delicacy! And, of
course, in Hawaii this is another
wonderful way to serve bananas,
as an appetizer.*

Karen Ledgerwood's Crab Meat Pizza is a colorful appetizer for the holidays.

Karen Ledgerwood comes from a very large family--11 brothers and 1 sister. Being the oldest girl, she became her mother's helper at an early age. She admits she is a good cook because of the years of training, but adds that some of her mother's talent may have rubbed off on her.

Ledgerwood received this recipe from a friend at the Welcome Wagon Club in Henderson, Kentucky. After moving to Hawaii, Ledgerwood, a research associate at the University of Hawaii, brought this dish to a family Christmas gathering in Pearl City. When asked what it was, she replied, "**Crab Meat Pizza**." She was given a strange look and no one touched it. After her children started eating it, others tried it and loved it. A couple of the aunts at the party even asked for the recipe.

6

Crab Meat Pizza

12 ounces cream cheese (or low-fat
    cream cheese)
2 tablespoons Worcestershire sauce
2 teaspoons lemon juice
2 tablespoons mayonnaise
1 small onion, minced
1 (12-ounce) bottle Heinz chili sauce
1 (6-ounce) can crab meat, drained
    and flaked
2 tablespoons parsley

Cream first 5 ingredients together
and spread in circle on a 12-inch
plate or platter. Pour chili sauce on
top and spread over surface.
Sprinkle crab meat on top of sauce,
then sprinkle entire pizza with
parsley. Refrigerate 3 hours before
serving. Serve with crackers.

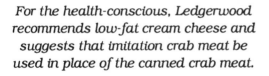

*For the health-conscious, Ledgerwood
recommends low-fat cream cheese and
suggests that imitation crab meat be
used in place of the canned crab meat.*

Advertiser **photo by Charles Okamura**
Lenora Lee created Shrimp Maunakea.

Lenora Lee needed an extra-special dish for a dinner she was planning. So she created **Shrimp Maunakea** with a peanut dip. The creation was a big hit with her guests, who were gourmet cooks.

Lee, a legal assistant with the Legal Aid Society, is working toward an MBA degree at Chaminade University of Honolulu. She and her husband, Douglas, have two sons in college.

Lee learned to cook only after her marriage, but has never forgotten the advice of a cooking instructor 26 years ago at the YWCA. The instructor told her to put love into her cooking, and Lee says that's what she has been doing all these years.

Shrimp Maunakea

1 pound large shrimp (about 20),
   cleaned, deveined
20 Chinese snow peas, blanched or
   microwaved until just tender
1 small bunch mint
1 small bunch basil
1 small bunch Chinese parsley
20 barbecue sticks

Peanut Dip:
2 tablespoons chunky peanut
   butter
3 tablespoons vinegar
1/4 cup soy sauce
1 tablespoon sugar
2 teaspoons fresh lime juice
1 mashed chili pepper
1 clove garlic, finely minced

Cook shrimp in 1 quart boiling water with 1 teaspoon salt added. Cook until shrimp turns pink, about 4 minutes. Do not overcook or the shrimp will be tough.

Wrap each shrimp around the middle with a basil leaf, a mint leaf, a sprig of Chinese parsley and, last, a Chinese snow pea. Then skewer on a barbecue stick.

Peanut Dip: Mix all ingredients together and serve the dip in a bowl with the skewered shrimp placed around the bowl on a platter.

Makes 4 to 6 servings.

Lee calls this dish Shrimp Maunakea because most of the spices and herbs can be obtained at the shops along Maunakea Street in Chinatown. When the shrimp is assembled, the colors of the pink shrimp, green, leafy herbs and bamboo skewers remind you of Bali and Thailand and also of Maunakea Street.

Diana Veach's Tofu Poke was tops in the appetizer category.

Diana Veach was totally surprised to learn that her **Tofu Poke** had won top honors in the "My Best Recipe" contest appetizer category. The judges were impressed with the way Veach had flavored the tofu, and how she managed to retain the freshness and crunchiness of the seaweed. Veach thinks the last-minute addition of grated ginger did the trick, helping to enhance the flavor.

A food service supervisor at Kuakini Medical Center, Veach enjoys creative cooking and is always thinking up new dishes like the poke dish. Although she's not a vegetarian, she enjoys creating menus using tofu and says it makes for enjoyable and ono recipes.

Tofu Poke

1 block firm tofu (cut into 1-inch
    cubes), drained
2 teaspoons toasted sesame seeds
1/4 cup coarsely chopped limu
    (seaweed)
2 tablespoons chopped green onion
1 teaspoon grated ginger
1/2 large red chili pepper, seeded
    and chopped
1/4 cup shoyu
1 tablespoon sesame oil

Place tofu cubes in a colander to
drain; then place in a serving bowl.
Sprinkle sesame seeds, limu,
chopped onion, ginger and chili
pepper over tofu cubes and toss
lightly.

Mix shoyu and sesame oil
together and pour over the rest of
the ingredients. Toss lightly and
chill for 1/2 hour.

---

*Using firm tofu that has been drained
well in the colander helps to keep the
dish from becoming watery and
tasteless. Veach also recommends
fresh limu (seaweed) to add
crunchiness to the poke.*

Helen Francell's Westport Room Salad has a rich, garlicky flavor.

For years, **Helen Francell** had to eat at Union Station's Westport Room in Kansas City, Missouri, to have her favorite salad, but when the restaurant closed over 25 years ago, the chef shared the recipe with a friend, who in turn gave it to Francell's mother.

Francell, who moved here four years ago, assists her husband, Garry, who is account representative for the Research Institute of America. She especially enjoys preparing vegetarian and Indian dishes. She likes to serve **Westport Room Salad** on special occasions like Thanksgiving or Christmas, but it can be served any time. Her friends love it and often ask for the recipe.

Westport Room Salad

1 head crisp Romaine lettuce
1 head iceberg lettuce
1/2 head cauliflower, grated
1 cup toasted buttered bread
    crumbs

Dressing:
1 cup mayonnaise (or low-
    cholesterol mayonnaise)
1/2 cup Parmesan cheese, grated
Juice of 1 lemon
1 clove garlic, crushed
Salt and pepper to taste
1/2 cup whipping cream (can use
    non-fat or low-fat milk) to thin
    dressing

For dressing, mix all the ingredients and thin with only as much cream or milk as needed.

Pour dressing into bowl of lettuce broken into bite-size pieces. Toss gently. Sprinkle with grated cauliflower. Top with bread crumbs.

You also can prepare the lettuce ahead and add the dressing, grated cauliflower and bread crumbs just before serving. Makes 8 hearty servings.

Margo Hill's Cream Cheese Jell-o® is refreshing as well as pretty.

Margo Hill's next-door neighbor gave her the recipe for **Cream Cheese Jell-o®** about 12 years ago. It takes little time to prepare, and friends always ask for the recipe.

Hill loves to cook and entertain. Formal parties are her specialty, and she enjoys using her fancy linen tablecloths and silver candelabra. She frequently entertains her daughter and family with elegant dinners.

Whenever she serves the Cream Cheese Jell-o®, she dresses it up by topping each piece with half a maraschino cherry.

The recipe is popular for picnics or potlucks, as it can be made the day before to save time.

14

Cream Cheese Jell-o®

1 small package lime Jell-o®
1 small package lemon Jell-o®
2 cups hot water
1 cup cold water
1 small package cream cheese
1 small can crushed pineapple,
    drained dry
3 tablespoons mayonnaise

Put both lime and lemon Jell-o® in an 8- by 8-inch Pyrex® dish. Add 2 cups hot water and stir well until completely dissolved. Add the cold water. Put dish in refrigerator to jell. In a bowl, add pineapple and mayonnaise to cream cheese and mix; then refrigerate.

When Jell-o® is almost jelled, remove from refrigerator. Add the cream mixture to the Jell-o® and mix well. Return to refrigerator.

When mixture is completely jelled, cut it into squares and serve on a dish lined with lettuce leaves. It can also be served as a dessert.

Advertiser **photo by T. Umeda**
Sherry Kilgore's Frozen Cranberry Salad is easy to make.

Sherry Kilgore's Frozen Cranberry Salad is a treasured recipe that has been handed down from her grandmother to her mother, and then to her. It's delicious and not too rich.

Kilgore said her children don't like cranberries, but when she puts them in the salad, they love it. The salad will keep for about 1-1/2 weeks in the freezer, but won't last that long once family members get a taste of it.

Kilgore, secretary to the vice-president for project development at Halekulani Corporation, her husband, Jerry, and their three children moved to Hawaii five years ago from Oklahoma City. They had vacationed in Hawaii before and liked it so much they sold their home and moved here for good.

Frozen
Cranberry Salad

13 ounces cream cheese
1 can whole berry cranberry sauce
1 cup Dream Whip®, prepared
14-ounce can crushed pineapple,
    drained
2 tablespoons sugar
1/2 to 3/4 cup chopped nuts

Soften cream cheese with cranberry
sauce and pineapple. Blend sugar
with prepared Dream Whip®. Mix
both mixtures together until
smooth; add nuts. Before putting
the mixture into a container, spray
the latter with nonstick vegetable oil
spray so the salad will be easier to
remove. Freeze. Serve like ice
cream or salad.

Ken Rakta created Broiled Salmon Salad with Raspberry Dressing.

Ken Rakta learned to cook out of necessity while attending Brigham Young University-Hawaii. Back home in Thailand, his mother taught cooking, so he enjoyed excellent meals. But when he arrived in Hawaii in 1965, there was no one to cook for him--he "had to learn to cook or starve," he said.

After graduation, he went into the food and beverage business. His **Broiled Salmon Salad with Raspberry Dressing**, which he created, always brings compliments from family and friends.

Clubhouse manager at Mid-Pacific Country Club, Rakta usually leaves cooking chores to his wife, Roann, but pitches in when they have company.

18

Broiled Salmon Salad with Raspberry Dressing

8- to 10-ounce fresh salmon filet
2 to 3 tablespoons any Italian
    dressing
1 head red leaf lettuce
1 head Romaine lettuce
6 medium-size fresh mushrooms
1 small bunch watercress
1/2 medium sweet onion (Maui or
    Texas Round)
1 large tomato

Dressing:
1/2 cup frozen raspberries (or
    raspberry preserves)
1/4 cup red wine vinegar
1/4 cup water
1/2 teaspoon chervil
1 tablespoon sugar
1/2 teaspoon salt
1 teaspoon lemon juice
1/2 teaspoon Grey Poupon®
    mustard
3/4 cup good olive oil

Skin the salmon filet and remove small bones with tweezers or small, long pliers. Marinate in Italian dressing for 1/2 hour. Broil on charcoal or gas broiler until done and let cool.

Wash and tear red leaf lettuce to bite-size pieces; wash and cut Romaine lettuce same size. Wash and cut watercress to 1-inch size; discard large, tough stem parts. Dice tomato and slice mushrooms and sweet onion.

Keep all salad ingredients chilled while preparing the dressing. Onion tastes sweeter when cold.

For dressing: Add water to red wine vinegar, add frozen raspberries and reduce on medium heat to 1/2 volume. Add chervil and let cool. Combine the above with salt, sugar, lemon juice and mustard while still lukewarm. After the liquid has cooled, whisk in olive oil slowly.

Combine salad ingredients and cut the salmon into about 1/2-inch squares. Toss lightly and add dressing slowly so as not to drench the salad. Add salmon and a few turns of fresh ground pepper last. Garnish with a sliced strawberry or a red bell pepper ring.

Sharon Thompson's salad has an Island flavor.

Sharon Thompson's brother-in-law, Robert Mandel, gave her this recipe when she visited him in Virginia last summer. "Robert has a flair for cooking," said Thompson, who came to Hawaii three years ago with her husband, Don, and two children. She works part-time in the Castle Medical Center Emergency Room, and he is an investigator with the navy.

"We've grown to love this place, but we have to leave next summer," said Thompson regretfully. "We enjoy the culture, weather, and food, especially the Asian dishes. You have some of the best restaurants here."

Robert's Sesame Asparagus Salad

2 to 3 pounds asparagus, crisply
  steamed (about 5 minutes
  with   stalks down)

Marinade:
2 to 3 garlic cloves, minced
5 to 6 tablespoons sesame seeds
Hot pepper flakes or fresh hot chili
  pepper to taste
2 to 3 teaspoons ground ginger
2 to 3 teaspoons Dijon mustard
1-1/4 cups olive oil
1/4 cup sesame oil
1/4 cup balsamic vinegar
1/4 cup soy sauce
2 to 3 tablespoons sherry

Roast minced garlic and sesame seeds for about 10 minutes in a 350-degree oven until golden brown. Mix with all ingredients and adjust for taste. Add asparagus to marinade and put in refrigerator for several hours. It can be made a day ahead.

The above salad makes a fine dish by itself, but to make the complete Oriental salad, place several asparagus stalks and about 2 to 3 tablespoons of the marinade on individual tossed salads made up of whatever mix of chopped raw Oriental vegetables are fresh at the market.

The following are recommended: bok choy, scallions, bean sprouts, radishes, pea pods, green pepper, mild red pepper and celery cabbage.

Entrées

Elizabeth Aulsebrook's Roast Beef and Romaine Salad is easy to prepare.

Elizabeth Aulsebrook adapted this recipe from a *Working Woman* article on winter salads. Her husband loves this salad with fresh french bread. Aulsebrook said it's a marvelous way to use leftover roast or steak and super easy to put together after a long day.

Aulsebrook suggests you double the recipe for a potluck dinner.

Roast Beef and Romaine Salad

1 large head Romaine lettuce
Honey Mustard Dressing (see recipe
   below)
1 pound cooked rare roast beef,
   steak, or chopped steak,
   cut into bite- size pieces
1/2-pound Monterey Jack cheese,
   cut into bite-size chunks
12 ounces unsalted walnuts or
   pecans, roughly broken
4 tablespoons chopped green onion

Honey Mustard Dressing:
4 tablespoons honey
4 tablespoons red-wine vinegar
4 tablespoons Dijon-style mustard
1/2 cup olive oil

Whisk all dressing ingredients together in a small bowl. Makes abut 1 cup.

Wash and dry the Romaine leaves and tear into pieces. Wrap in a tea towel in the refrigerator for up to several hours. Toss lettuce in a bowl with a small amount of Honey Mustard Dressing.

   In a small bowl, toss the steak with enough dressing to coat lightly. Combine all ingredients and toss gently. Serve with extra dressing for those who prefer more. Serves 4 as a main course.

A glass of Zinfandel goes well with this.

Advertiser **photo by Carl Viti**

Jimmi Campbell's Spam® Skillet Salad is tasty, colorful and very easy to prepare.

Jimmi Campbell's Spam® Skillet Salad came all the way from Trion, Georgia. She thinks she obtained the recipe from a friend about 30 years ago, and over the years it has become a family favorite. She used to make the salad for her granddaughter Emily in South Carolina, but now that Campbell lives in Hawaii, Emily makes the salad for herself.

Campbell's husband is state overseer of Churches of God Denomination, with headquarters in Cleveland, Tennessee. Being a pastor's wife, Campbell often entertains. Her favorite party dishes are casseroles and salads.

26

Spam® Skillet Salad

1/2 cup chopped fresh green onions
1/2 cup chopped green peppers
1 (12-ounce) can of Spam®, chopped
1 tablespoon oil
3 medium potatoes, boiled and
    diced
1/4 teaspoon salt
1/4 teaspoon black pepper
1/4 cup mayonnaise
1/2 pound sharp cheese, diced

Cook onions, pepper and meat in hot oil, stirring occasionally until meat is lightly browned. Add potatoes, salt, pepper and mayonnaise. Heat this mixture very lightly. Stir in cheese; heat just until it begins to melt. Pour onto a platter and garnish with fresh green onions and green pepper rings or either one.

Green beans and rolls are a nice accompaniment to this salad.

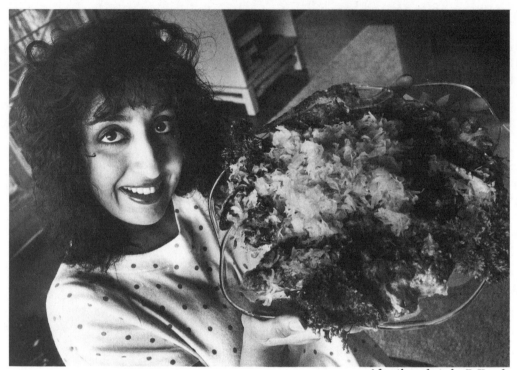

Carole Desaulniers with her Country-Style Pork Ribs With Sauerkraut.

Whenever **Carole Desaulniers** takes her **Country-Style Pork Ribs With Sauerkraut** to potluck parties, it's a big hit. She said this dish is not only easy to prepare, but looks as if she spent hours in the kitchen preparing it.

Desaulniers, who works full-time at her husband Stephen's glass-tinting company, said this recipe is great for people who are constantly on the go and are exhausted at the end of the day. She has changed the basic recipe by adding wine, which makes it taste even better. The dish has a sweet-sour effect.

Desaulniers learned gourmet cooking from her father, who owned an Italian restaurant in Houston, Texas, and home-style cooking from her mother. She has also learned to combine and create her own dishes.

Country-Style Pork Ribs with Sauerkraut

6 to 8 thick country-style pork ribs
3/4 cup chicken broth
1 (32-ounce) jar sauerkraut,
    drained well
2 to 3 teaspoons brown sugar
3 tablespoons butter or margarine
3 tablespoons olive oil (or other
    vegetable oil)
1/2 cup dry white wine
1/2 cup flour
Ground black pepper, Italian herbs,
    garlic powder to taste

Pour jar of sauerkraut into a sieve in the sink and let it drain well. While it is draining, sprinkle ribs with pepper, garlic powder and Italian herbs and coat with flour. Heat oil in frying pan on medium heat and lightly brown ribs.

Transfer to a deep stew pot. Add chicken broth, wine, and drained sauerkraut and sprinkle with brown sugar and dot with butter. Salt and pepper to taste. Simmer on low heat for 1 to 1-1/2 hours, or until meat falls from bone. Serve with mashed potatoes.

Advertiser **photo by Charles Okamura**
Nita Hogue's Beef Stroganoff is a great dish for company.

Nita Hogue can always depend on her **Beef Stroganoff** when she needs a party dish. The recipe was given to her by a friend 30 years ago and it's been in her files ever since.

Originally from Canada, Hogue moved to Hawaii 14 years ago when her husband, Guy, was transferred here by his company. She manages The Framery, Ltd., in Kilohana Square, which is owned by her two sons.

Hogue and her husband try to stick to a low-fat diet now that their children have left home. She does a lot of stir-frys using vegetables, but says the stroganoff is great once in a while when expecting company.

Beef Stroganoff

1-1/2 pounds beef tenderloin or
    sirloin (well trimmed and cut in
    wedges)
2 or 3 cans of mushrooms or fresh
    mushrooms browned with the
    meat
1 large round onion, coarsely
    chopped
1 (8-ounce) container sour cream or
    low-fat yogurt
2 or 3 bouillon cubes
Lemon juice (about 1/2 lemon)
1 teaspoon spicy mustard
Pepper to taste
1-1/2 teaspoons salt or to taste
Paprika to taste
1 tablespoon catsup

The spices are what make this dish so special. Try low-fat yogurt in place of sour cream if you're conscious of calories. A salad and bread are all that are needed to complete this dish.

Brown meat in butter. Add about 2 cups of water and the bouillon cubes. Cook about 1/2 hour or until meat is tender.

Add chopped or sliced onion and cook until just tender. Add mushrooms, catsup, mustard, other spices and enough water to almost cover. Cook just a few minutes and add sour cream. The mixture can be thickened with flour or cornstarch if desired. Serve over noodles, fresh pasta or rice.

Advertiser **photo by Carl Viti**

Lori Kutara's Ono Meat Loaf is tasty and very simple to make.

Lori Kutara, mother of three and a full-time employee at Central Pacific Bank, has a hectic schedule, but has learned to set priorities. She tries to be cautious about what she serves her family, but says she's not overly strict.

Kutara says she disliked meat loaf until a good friend taught her how to make this special meat loaf, a family favorite.

The "My Best Recipe" contest judges thought the minced clams in Kutara's meat loaf added just enough flavor to enhance the taste, with the mushroom gravy giving it the finishing touch.

Ono Meat Loaf

1 pound ground beef
1/2 to 3/4 pound ground pork
1 (6 1/2-ounce) can minced clams
   (set aside liquid)
1 package Lipton Onion Soup Mix
1/2 carrot, grated
2 stalks celery, chopped
1 egg
Pepper to taste
Dash garlic salt
2 cloves garlic, grated
2 slices whole wheat bread

Gravy:
1 (4-ounce) can sliced mushrooms
   (save liquid)
1 can cream of mushroom soup

Soak bread slices in clam juice. Mix together all ingredients. Shape into a loaf in a 13- by 9-inch pan and bake in a 375-degree oven for 45 minutes to 1 hour.

For gravy, mix together sliced mushrooms, including the liquid, with cream of mushroom soup. Pour mixture over loaf the last 15 minutes and continue baking, basting often until gravy turns brown.

Advertiser **photo by Richard Ambo**

Marian Myers' nickname is Merv; hence the name Veal à la Merv.

Marian Myers did not learn to cook until she got married. But once she started to experiment with a variety of recipes, she really began to enjoy cooking. She loves to bake bread using yeast and especially likes the kneading part.

Myers and her husband, Arthur, live in Hawaii Kai and have three sons. She enjoys looking through magazines for tips on gourmet cooking and has a roomful of cookbooks. She is always looking for good recipes, since her family doesn't eat out much.

Her family enjoys veal scallopini and veal Parmesan. So when she found recipes for each with some of the same basic ingredients, Myers decided to combine the two, adding some of the other ingredients from each recipe, plus one or two ingredients of her own.

34

Veal à la Merv

3 pounds veal steak (1/4- to 1/3-
   inch thick)
1/2 cup flour
1 teaspoon salt
Dash pepper
1/2 teaspoon garlic powder
1 teaspoon paprika
1/2 cup cracker meal or dry bread
   crumbs
1/4 cup grated Parmesan cheese
1 tablespoon butter
2 tablespoons olive or vegetable oil
1-1/2 cups fresh mushrooms, sliced
1/4 cup green pepper, chopped
1 beef bouillon cube
1 (16-ounce) can tomato sauce
1/2 cup dry vermouth
1-1/2 tablespoons oregano
2 cups grated mozzarella cheese

Pound the meat thoroughly with a meat pounder or heavy knife. Cut into serving pieces. Combine the flour, salt, pepper, garlic powder, paprika, cracker meal and Parmesan cheese. Coat meat with mixture.

Heat butter and oil in a large skillet and brown the meat on each side. More oil can be added if necessary. When the meat is browned, remove from pan and place in a dish. Set aside.

In same skillet, over low heat, cook the mushrooms and green peppers (about 5 minutes). Dissolve the bouillon cube in 1/2 cup of boiling water and pour into skillet. Add the tomato sauce, vermouth and oregano.

Return the meat to the skillet and add 1-1/2 cups of mozzarella cheese. Cover; simmer the meat for 1 hour, stirring occasionally. More vermouth can be added if sauce becomes too thick. Place meat and sauce on serving platter and sprinkle with remaining 1/2 cup of mozzarella cheese. Garnish with parsley. Serve with noodles or rice.

_____

Myers like this recipe because it can be made in advance. Chicken breasts, skinned and boned, can be substituted for the veal.

_____

Pam Stair's Japanese Lasagna is a one-dish meal, served right from the pan.

Pam Stair's recipe for **Japanese Lasagna** came all the way from Yokosuka Naval Base in Japan, where her husband, Bradley, was stationed with the navy for 13 years. A Japanese friend gave Stair the recipe, and her family liked it. Different but delicious, the dish is easy to make--just put all the ingredients into a frying pan and cook for a few minutes.

Stair, who speaks Japanese well, came to the Islands a little over a year ago with her husband and children. They are stationed at Barbers Point. She prefers to prepare simple dishes, such as casseroles, and loves to bake.

36

Japanese Lasagna

3 or 4 slices of bacon
1 medium-size onion, sliced and
    separated into rings
1 large potato, sliced
1 medium-size eggplant, sliced
About 1 cup uncooked macaroni,
    ribbon or other fancy shapes,
    to cover mixture.
1-pound jar or 1-pound can meat
    sauce or your own family recipe
Mozzarella cheese, 8-ounce-size
    package or more

In a large frying pan, layer the above ingredients, except cheese, in the order given. Cover and cook over medium heat until it reaches the boiling stage. Reduce heat to low and cook 10 to 15 minutes or until the vegetables are tender. Add slices of mozzarella to cover mixture. Cover and heat 2 or 3 minutes longer, or until cheese is melted. Serve from the pan.

Advertiser photo by Charles Okamura

Dorothy Steele's Thin Veal Forestier has a touch of lemon and vermouth.

Dorothy Steele believes that her recipe for **Thin Veal Forestier** is more than 50 years old. It originated with her late grandmother-in-law and was passed down from one generation to another. She likes the recipe because it is elegant and easy to prepare and she always receives raves and requests for the recipe.

Steele says her husband's mother, Mona, was an outstanding cook and probably is most responsible for her interest in cooking and in collecting recipes.

Steele, who works at Punahou School's Cooke Library, said the veal dish has been enjoyed in Kansas, California, Missouri, California, Texas and Hawaii, her home since 1966.

Thin Veal Forestier

1-1/2 pounds thin veal steak
Cut clove garlic
Flour
1/4 cup butter or margarine
1/2 teaspoon salt
Dash pepper
1/3 cup dry vermouth
1 teaspoon lemon juice
1/2 pound thinly sliced fresh
    mushrooms
Snipped parsley

Flatten veal to 1/4-inch thickness. Cut into 2-inch pieces. Rub both sides of each piece with garlic; sprinkle with flour. In hot butter or margarine sauté veal, several pieces at a time in skillet, until golden brown on both sides.

Heap mushrooms on top of all pieces in skillet. Sprinkle with salt, pepper and vermouth. Cook, covered, over low heat 20 minutes, or until veal is fork tender, checking occasionally to make sure it is moist; if not, add about 1 tablespoon of water. To serve, sprinkle with lemon juice and parsley. Serves 6.

Advertiser photo by Gregory Yamamoto

Tina Apana's Tofu-Turkey Balls are a nutritious family favorite.

With two teen-age boys in the family, **Tina Apana** is always looking for hearty, healthy recipes. Sometimes she creates her own dishes to make them more nutritious--like her **Tofu-Turkey Balls**.

Apana said her husband, Mel, loves tofu, but their sons hate it so she thought up this recipe. The combination of ground turkey and tofu did the trick.

Apana, a baker at Marie Callender's Restaurant & Bakeries, says she's always enjoyed cooking. Since she had a working mom, she learned to cook while caring for her grandfather.

Tofu-Turkey Balls

1/2 pound ground turkey
12 ounces tofu, mashed and
    drained
1 egg
1/2 onion, finely chopped
1/4 cup bread crumbs
2 tablespoons sherry
1/4 cup chopped green onions
1 cup panko bread crumbs
Salt and pepper to taste
Oil for frying

Teri Sauce:
2 tablespoons cornstarch
1/4 cup sugar
1/3 cup soy sauce
2 tablespoons sherry
1 clove garlic, crushed
1 teaspoon grated fresh ginger

Combine turkey, tofu, egg, onion, bread crumbs, sherry, green onions and salt and pepper. Mix well. Form into 1-inch meat balls; roll into panko. Drop meatballs into hot oil and fry until golden brown. Serve with teriyaki dipping sauce.

    Teri sauce: In small saucepan, combine ingredients and cook until thickened. Serve with rice or pasta.

Junne Barnes with her Mexican dish, Aztec Pudding.

Junne Barnes' Norwegian relatives love to cook, so she was exposed to fine cooking at an early age. She's a whiz at preparing Norwegian dishes, but submitted this Mexican recipe called **Aztec Pudding** because it's more appropriate here in Hawaii.

Barnes got the recipe for this casserole from a friend many years ago. She says you can add the chilies according to your taste--if you like your food mild, add fewer chilies, and if you like it hot, add more.

Barnes, a professional puppeteer and an actress, has had parts in "Magnum, P.I." and "Island Son," both filmed here.

42

Aztec Pudding

4 skinless chicken breasts (can use
    turkey leftovers)
1 dozen corn tortillas
1 can cream of chicken soup
1 can cream of mushroom soup
1 (4-ounce) can green chilies
    (seeded and cut in strips; can
    use less)
1 (4-ounce) can sliced black olives
1 cup milk
1 medium onion, minced
1/2 to 3/4 pound cheddar cheese,
    grated

Wrap chicken breasts in foil and bake 1 hour in 375-degree oven. Cool, then cut into bite-sized pieces. Save the stock for the casserole.

Cut tortillas into quarters. Mix together soups, green chilies, milk and onion. Butter at least 3-quart casserole and put stock on bottom. Layer ingredients as follows: tortilla pieces, chicken, soup mixture, olives and grated cheese. (Use as much cheese as you like.) Top with olives. Refrigerate for 24 hours before baking. Bake at 300 degrees for 1 hour.

George Curtis' Madras-Style Curry in a pineapple is baked in the oven.

George Curtis travels a lot so he picks up ideas and adapts them to his style of cooking. For the "My Best Recipe" contest he came up with a unique pineapple container to hold his **Madras-Style Curry**.

Curtis, who does ocean-related research and teaches at the University of Hawaii's College of Engineering, says he and his brother learned to cook when they were teen-agers. They cooked because they got hungry waiting for their mother to return from her golf games.

Since coming to Hawaii 25 years ago, Curtis has been experimenting with grilled food and Mexican dishes. He claims his wife, Jean, is the expert when it comes to cooking.

Madras-Style Curry

2 tablespoons margarine
1/2 onion, chopped
3 tablespoons curry powder (vary to
    taste)
1 tablespoon flour
1/2 cup plain yogurt
1/2 apple, peeled and diced
1/4 cup raisins
1 tablespoon sugar
Salt to taste
About 1 cup cooked chicken,
    shrimp, etc., in chunks
1 medium pineapple

In frying pan, melt margarine and lightly fry onions and curry powder to bring out the flavor. Add flour, then yogurt and simmer about 5 minutes, stirring for a smooth sauce. Add all other ingredients, correct seasonings and simmer at least 15 minutes. Thin with water or chicken broth if necessary as sauce thickens.

Cut top from pineapple and make a cavity for the filling. Add some of the fruit that was removed and the juice to the curry. Pour the entire mixture into the pineapple cavity. Put a pan under the pineapple in case the curry overflows. Bake at 350 degrees for 1/2 hour.

Serve over rice with chutney and condiments such as crushed peanuts, bacon bits, raisins, chopped chives and coconut.

Curtis first made a sort of curry from leftover chicken and a container of pineapple yogurt. When he tried out a new pineapple corer, he decided to use some of the fruit in the curry. He baked it in the shell and it worked fine, making a nice service as well as adding flavor.

Advertiser **photo by Charles Okamura**
Don Fields has added local flavors to his Southwestern Chicken with Tomato Papaya Salsa.

Don Fields took a semi-professional cooking course in Boston 10 years ago because he thought seriously about going into the restaurant business. But he ended up in a totally unrelated job as management consultant with Ernst and Young CPAs.

Fields said his cooking instructor in Boston used to make a great variation of Chicken Cordon Bleu by coating the chicken in ground almonds instead of bread crumbs. Fields, originally from Texas, likes spicy Southwestern food. He adapted his cooking instructor's recipe, substituting pecans and blue corn meal for the almonds, and using smoked cheese and scallions for the filling. Fields grew up on regular Mexican salsa, but likes making up a more Hawaiian-style salsa using the ginger, papaya and lime juice.

46

Southwestern Chicken with Tomato Papaya Salsa

2 large chicken breasts, split (four pieces), skins and bones removed
2 tablespoons shredded smoked gouda cheese
2 scallions, chopped
1/2 cup blue (or yellow) corn meal
1/2 cup pecans
1 egg
1 tablespoon water
3/4 cup flour
Salt and pepper
Cooking oil or butter

Salsa:
2 cups ripe tomatoes, peeled, seeded and chopped
1 cup ripe chopped papaya
1 fresh jalapeño pepper, seeded and finely chopped
1/2 tablespoon minced fresh ginger
1/4 cup scallions, chopped
1-1/2 tablespoons (small bunch) basil, roughly chopped
1/4 to 1/2 cup water
Lime juice

Prepare chicken breasts by placing flat on work surface and slicing a pocket in each breast about half the depth of the breast. Sprinkle inside of pocket with salt and pepper, about a teaspoon of scallions and some of the cheese. Seal pocket by rubbing with finger. If there are tears in the chicken, the coating below will seal them.

Prepare coating by grinding pecans in a food processor until very fine. Mix pecans with blue corn meal and a dash of salt and pepper in a wide, shallow bowl. Mix flour with a dash of salt and pepper and place on a piece of wax paper. Beat egg and water together in a small bowl.

Lightly flour each breast, patting off excess. Brush with the egg mixture and then dip in cornmeal/pecan mixture, making sure the sides are covered. Pat off any excess. Set aside. This can be made the day before and refrigerated.

Prepare salsa by mixing all ingredients together except the water. Be careful with the jalapeño; they vary in intensity, so add according to taste. Add only enough water to obtain the right consistency for salsa; then add lime juice to taste. Simmer the salsa until warm, but do not boil.

Heat the oil in a heavy skillet and cook the chicken breasts until firm to the touch and lightly browned. Place on a plate and spoon warm salsa over. Serve with sliced, blanched yams sautéed with lime, nutmeg and butter, and with refried black beans.

This salsa is also great on grilled or sautéed fish.

Irene Higuchi shares her family's Baked Parmesan Chicken recipe.

Irene T. Higuchi's family of four children and 10 grandchildren enjoys all types of food--from miso soup to pizza. But Higuchi, a retired widow from the plantation community of Lahaina, Maui, loves Japanese food best of all. Since moving to Aiea about 12 years ago, Higuchi has made her home with her daughter, Lorraine Saari, her husband, Raymond, and their two young children.

Saari says the kids love their grandma's cooking, especially the Japanese dishes, which are either done the old-fashioned way or Island-style.

Higuchi, who got this recipe from her sister, says she has always enjoyed cooking and now collects good recipes.

Baked Parmesan Chicken

4 chicken breasts, deboned and
    flattened
1/2 cup Parmesan cheese, grated
2 eggs, well beaten
3/4 cup plain bread crumbs (or
    Kellogg's cornflakes crumbs,
    which Higuchi prefers)
1/4 to 1/2 cup cooking oil
Butter or margarine to sauté
    mushrooms
1/2 pound fresh mushrooms or
    1 can drained large mushrooms
1/2 cup white cooking wine
4 slices Monterey Jack cheese

Get three separate bowls for the grated Parmesan cheese, the eggs and the bread crumbs. Dip flattened chicken breasts in grated cheese first, then the eggs and the bread crumbs.

Brown chicken in oil; then place in baking pan. Do not overlap chicken. Place a slice of Monterey Jack cheese on each breast.

A half hour before serving, sauté sliced mushrooms in butter or margarine and add wine. Place mushrooms on each breast and pour the liquid from the mushroom-wine mixture over each.

Bake covered in 325-degree oven for 30 minutes and no longer or it will dry up the chicken. Garnish with chopped parsley and lemon juice.

Joan Kreeger's delicious Chicken Florentine is low in calories and cholesterol.

Joan Kreeger's husband, Richard, discovered the recipe for **Chicken Florentine** in a magazine about a year ago. Friends and family--even Kreeger's 12-year-old son--love it.

Kreeger, a social worker with the Department of Health, came to Hawaii from Maryland 22 years ago and liked it so much she decided to stay. She also met her husband here. She explained that both she and her husband enjoy cooking. "My husband experiments a lot, but I don't have the patience. I like things that are quick and foolproof. Lately, we have been changing our eating habits to include healthier food, such as more skinless chicken and less red meat."

Chicken Florentine

1/2 cup diced onion
1 clove garlic
1/2 cup chopped mushrooms
1/2 cup cooked chopped spinach
1/2 cup part skim ricotta cheese
1/2 teaspoon salt
1/4 teaspoon oregano leaves
1/4 teaspoon pepper
4 chicken breast halves, pounded to
    1/4-inch thick
4 teaspoons reduced calorie
    margarine
3 to 4 tablespoons Italian dried
    bread crumbs
3 tablespoons dry white wine

Preheat oven to 350 degrees. Sauté onion, garlic and mushrooms in nonstick vegetable oil spray in skillet. Remove from heat and stir in spinach, cheese, 1/4 teaspoon salt, 1/4 teaspoon oregano and 1/8 teaspoon pepper. Sprinkle chicken with 1/4 teaspoon salt and the remaining 1/8 teaspoon pepper.

Spread spinach mixture onto chicken, leaving a 1/2-inch border on each. Roll closed and secure with skewers. Place chicken in 11- by 7-inch baking dish that has been coated with nonstick vegetable oil spray.

Combine bread crumbs with melted margarine and sprinkle over chicken. Pour wine into baking dish; cover with foil and bake 20 minutes at 350 degrees. Remove foil and bake until crumbs are browned.

Advertiser photo by T. Umeda

Bill Lee's Shoyu Chicken and Noodles is good for potluck parties.

When it comes to home cooking, **Bill Lee** thinks he may have followed in his father's footsteps. He says he does all the cooking, just as his dad did. Lee says his wife wants to help, but he doesn't want her in the kitchen. He'd rather do everything himself.

Semi-retired since 1984 from the Board of Water Supply, where he was with the engineering section, Lee said he's a fanatic when it comes to cooking and collecting cookbooks. He has a room full of cookbooks, like a library. Lee tells his friends jokingly that domestic engineering is his profession.

Lee likes to cook low-fat and low-cholesterol dishes like **Shoyu Chicken and Noodles**, which is healthful as well as a favorite among his friends.

52

Shoyu Chicken and Noodles

5 pounds chicken thighs
1/2 cup shoyu
3 tablespoons sugar
1 tablespoon oyster sauce
3 tablespoons sherry wine
1/4 teaspoon ajinomoto (optional)
2 cloves garlic, crushed
1 thumb ginger, crushed
1 package udon

In a large pot, bring to boil all ingredients except chicken thighs. Add chicken thighs, deboned and skins removed if desired. Simmer about 45 minutes or less, depending on size of thighs. Make slits on both sides of bone to let sauce penetrate easily.

While chicken is simmering, boil one package of udon (Japanese noodles) according to directions. Drain, spread udon on platter and place chicken thighs over it. Thicken remaining gravy with cornstarch and water and pour over thighs. Sprinkle with Chinese parsley or green onion.

_____

Lee likes to blanch bean sprouts and place them over the noodles before topping with the chicken thighs. This gives it a crunchy flavor.

_____

Hazel Scott's Chicken Breasts Piquant is simple and delicious.

Hazel Scott prefers simple but tasty meals that don't take forever to prepare. **Chicken Breasts Piquant** is such a simple recipe that one of Scott's friends called her three times to make sure she hadn't omitted anything.

Scott, whose mother was a good cook, has been cooking since she was 12. A former secretary and also a police officer during World War II, she has traveled and worked in many parts of the world. She came to Hawaii in 1984. She had been visiting her sister and friends here for many years and decided it was time to move here permanently.

Scott enjoys having lunch with other seniors at Lanakila Multi-Purpose Senior Center five days a week. For a nominal fee, they are served healthful, economical and low-calorie dishes.

Chicken Breasts Piquant

3/4 cup rosé wine
1/4 cup soy sauce
1/4 cup olive oil
2 tablespoons water
1 clove garlic, sliced
1 teaspoon powdered ginger
1/4 teaspoon oregano
1 tablespoon brown sugar
3 chicken breasts, split in half
    (skinned if you prefer)

Combine wine, soy sauce, oil, water, garlic, ginger, oregano and brown sugar. Arrange chicken in baking dish; pour wine mixture over top. Cover and bake in moderate oven at 350 to 375 degrees about 1-1/2 hours, until tender.

You can use frozen chicken, but there will be more liquid in the sauce.

Serve over white, brown or wild rice (or a mixture). Makes 6 servings.

Holly Turner's Turkey Crèpes en Casserole is a dish fit for company.

Holly Turner, a nutrition major and a full-time mother of three children, says this dish with an elegant flair is especially great for an adult sit-down dinner. According to Turner, one advantage is that the casserole can be made ahead of the party. Then just pour the sauce over the crèpes casserole before heating it up.

Turner suggests you serve a fruit salad, cranberry sauce or tossed green salad with **Turkey Crèpes en Casserole**. This is one of Turner's favorite company dishes because it's a wonderful blend of flavors and textures and can be conveniently made ahead.

Turkey Crèpes en Casserole

Crèpes:
1 egg, beaten
1 cup milk
1 tablespoon melted butter
1 cup flour

Filling:
1 cup finely diced turkey
1/2 cup frozen spinach, thawed and
    drained
1 (10-3/4-ounce) can chicken soup
1/4 cup crushed saltines
1/4 cup sharp cheddar cheese,
    shredded
1/4 cup finely chopped onion

Crèpes: Beat the egg, milk and flour together until smooth; add melted butter. Refrigerate overnight.

Lightly grease a 6-inch skillet or crèpe pan. Heat over medium heat. Drop in 2 tablespoons batter. Roll the skillet to spread the batter thin. Set for 1 minute. Turn with fingers carefully and cook for 20 seconds on the second side. Makes 12 crèpes.

Filling: combine turkey, spinach, 1/2 cup chicken soup, saltines, cheese and onion. Put heaping tablespoon of filling on unbrowned side of each crèpe. Roll and arrange in 13- by 9-inch shallow baking dish, with the crease side down. Refrigerate if desired.

Pour over this the remaining 1/2 cup chicken soup mixed with 1 cup milk. Sprinkle with slivered almonds. Bake at 350 degrees for 30 minutes.

Advertiser photo by **Charles Okamura**

Jennie Wong's Stir-Fry Chicken Vegetables is an old family recipe.

In the old days, **Jennie Wong**'s grandmother, Ah Po, who passed on this recipe, used Chinese peas and dried mushrooms, but they're so expensive today that Wong substitutes canned button mushrooms and frozen peas and carrots. The juice from canned abalone also was used in the original dish, but Wong points out that not many can afford it now.

Wong has changed the recipe somewhat by using ingredients that are available in local markets, but there's no substitute for chicken. She says some people use ham or char siu (Chinese barbecued pork), but you can't duplicate the flavor.

Now that she's a grandmother, Wong is passing down this recipe to her daughters and other family members and hopes to pass it on to her granddaughter some day.

Stir-Fry Chicken Vegetables

1 pound chicken breasts, cut 3/4-
    inch by 1/4-inch thick
2 tablespoons soy sauce
1 tablespoon dry sherry
1 teaspoon sesame oil
2 tablespoons cornstarch
2 tablespoons peanut oil or salad oil
1 clove garlic, crushed
1 teaspoon fresh ginger, crushed
1/2 teaspoon sugar
1 medium-size round onion, diced
1 medium-size can bamboo shoots,
    diced
1/2 cup or 6 whole water chestnuts,
    diced
1 cup frozen peas, thawed
1 cup frozen carrots, thawed
1 small green pepper, diced
1 small can button mushrooms,
    whole, or stems and pieces
1 teaspoon soy sauce
1 teaspoon oyster sauce
2 tablespoons chicken broth
1 tablespoon cornstarch with 2
    tablespoons water and 1
    teaspoon sugar

Marinate the chicken with soy sauce, sherry and sesame oil. Coat the chicken pieces with 2 tablespoons cornstarch. Let stand for 15 minutes.

Heat 1 tablespoon oil in wok, and brown ginger and garlic in medium heat. Stir-fry the chicken for 3 to 5 minutes until golden brown. Remove from wok.

Heat 1 tablespoon oil. Brown onions; stir-fry 1 minute. Sprinkle with salt and sugar. Add bamboo shoots, water chestnuts, peas and carrots. Stir-fry 1 minute. Season with soy sauce and oyster sauce. Add green peppers and mushrooms. Season with soy sauce and sugar.

Return stir-fried chicken to the wok. Mix well with the cooked vegetables. Add broth and cornstarch mixture. Heat and stir until sauce thickens and boils.

Serve in the same wok, garnished with sprigs of Chinese parsley, and add 2 tablespoons chopped fried peanuts if desired. Serves 4 to 6.

Wong recommends this dish to brown-baggers, because most of it can be prepared overnight and the vegetables added at the last minute before leaving the house.

Advertiser **photo by Charles Okamura**
Judith Beasley with her favorite, Eggplant on Parade.

Judith Beasley learned to cook from her mother and grandmother while growing up in Tennessee. Her grandmother made her own biscuits and cornbread and even canned fresh vegetables grown in her garden. Her mother taught her how to make desserts, and Beasley won several badges for her cooking while a member of a Girl Scout troop.

An editorial assistant for the National Marine Fisheries Service,

Beasley said her eggplant recipe is simple. She tosses all the ingredients into a casserole dish and forgets about it until dinnertime. Lately, she has become more health-conscious and has been substituting brown rice for white rice in the dish.

Beasley says, "This recipe is one I found in a cookbook sent from Tennessee by my roommate's mother."

Eggplant on Parade

1 large or 3 small eggplants
3 beef bouillon cubes
1 medium onion, chopped
1 small bell pepper, chopped
2 stalks celery, chopped
1 tablespoon margarine
2 drops Tabasco® sauce
2 cups hot water
1 cup raw rice (white or brown)
1/2 to 1 pound cooked fresh
   shrimp, or 1 can shrimp,
   drained

Peel eggplant; cut in pieces. Cook in small amount of water until tender; drain. Dissolve bouillon cubes in hot water; fry onion, pepper and celery until transparent. Remove from heat; add remaining ingredients. Place in buttered two-quart casserole; cover and bake at 375 degrees for 1 hour and 15 minutes. Serves 6.

This recipe features three Hawaii favorites: eggplant, shrimp, and rice.

Dorsey Brady's Paella DRB is a great party dish.

Dorsey Brady, vice-president of operations for Outrigger Hotels Hawaii, has revised his **Paella DRB** dish many times since he first discovered it some 25 years ago in a *Playboy* cookbook. Brady says it's a Basque sheepherder dish in which you can substitute a variety of meats and seafoods--just use what tastes good to you.

Cooking is a hobby for Brady, who has been in the restaurant business for 27 years. He has been cooking since his high school days back in California, where he worked in beach concessions.

Brady says this dish is even better when moistened with some chicken broth and reheated the second day.

62

Paella DRB

2 pounds chicken thighs and
   breasts, cut into pieces
1/4 cup olive oil
1/4 cup water
1 onion, chopped
1 green pepper, chopped
2 garlic cloves, minced
2-1/4 cups uncooked rice
1 teaspoon saffron
4 cups chicken broth
1 pound cooked shrimp
1/2 pound Spanish chorizo
15 small clams
1 package frozen peas
1 small package frozen artichoke
   hearts
1 (4-ounce) can pimentos
4 ounces pork loin, cut into 1-inch
   squares
4 ounces veal loin, cut into 1-inch
   squares
Dry white wine

Heat oil in large skillet. Add pork
and chorizo and sauté lightly until
almost done. Remove from pan.
Add veal and chicken pieces and
brown all over. Add dry white wine
just to moisten, cover and simmer
30 minutes. Remove veal and
chicken and set aside.

In the same skillet, add onion
and garlic; sauté until clear. Add
rice and saffron; cook over low heat
until rice is light brown. Add
chicken broth, bring to a boil, cover,
reduce heat and simmer about 17
minutes.

Return rice, veal, pork, chicken,
shrimp, chorizo, pepper, pimento
and clams to skillet and blend
thoroughly. Put peas, artichoke
hearts and water in mixture and
cover. Simmer for 15 to 20 minutes.
Add more chicken broth if needed.
Rice should soak up most of the
broth. Taste for needed seasonings
and desired texture of rice. Finish
accordingly. Clams should be open
when done. Discard unopened
clams.

Note: The meat and vegetables
can be cut early in the day and can
be stored in the refrigerator until
time to cook.

---

*Paella DRB goes great with a simple
green salad and garlic bread. Brady
suggests a light red or a dry white
wine to accompany it.*

Thelma Edo's Clams with Black Bean Sauce is simple and tasty.

Thelma Edo of Kahului, Maui, is a single parent who has better things to do than slave over a hot stove. This mother of two says that these days she sets priorities so she can enjoy her time. Currently a secretary with Maui Electric Co., Edo, like all working mothers, was a fast-food cook when her children were younger. She made Chinese dishes because they were the easiest to prepare. This clam recipe may sound like lots of work, but it's simple to make and clams are available all year round.

She found the recipe in a Chinese cookbook but changed it slightly to make it simple and quick to do.

64

Clams with Black Bean Sauce

1 to 1-1/2 pounds clams
1 clove garlic, crushed
1 slice ginger, crushed
2 tablespoons oil
1 heaping teaspoon hot black bean
    sauce
2 teaspoons shoyu
1 tablespoon mirin
1 tablespoon rice wine
1/2 teaspoon salt
1 green onion, chopped
Some cornstarch for thickening

Soak, rinse and drain clams. Heat oil in wok until hot, add crushed ginger and garlic, and stir-fry a few seconds. Add clams and stir fry a few seconds.

Add soy sauce, mirin, rice wine, salt and about 1/3 cup water. Cover, bring to a full boil and steam until clams open up (about 3 minutes). Add green onions and thicken with cornstarch and water to desired consistency.

Prudence Lezy's prize-winning entrée Shrimp Lezy.

For **Prudence Lezy**, the four years she spent perfecting **Shrimp Lezy** paid off. Her dish was the winner in the entrée category in the 1990 My Best Recipe Contest.

An Air Force wife, she and her husband, Col. Norman G. Lezy, arrived from Washington, D.C., in 1987 and live at Hickam Air Force Base.

Lezy, a nutrition instructor in special education at Radford High School, says her recipe is a success wherever they go and she's glad she can share it with the state of Hawaii the second time around. During their stay in San Antonio, Texas, the Lezys came across a dish called Shrimp Paesano at an Italian restaurant and enjoyed it so much they asked for the recipe. But since the restaurant wouldn't share it, Lezy spent four years perfecting her own version.

Shrimp Lezy

16 (about 1 pound) jumbo shrimp
1 cup half and half or light cream
1 cup all-purpose flour
1 cup vegetable oil

Sauce:
Juice of 1/2 lemon (1-1/2
    tablespoons)
1 egg yolk
1/4 teaspoon ground white pepper
1/2 teaspoon salt
2 cloves garlic, peeled and minced
8 tablespoons chilled butter (must
    be butter)
1 tablespoon minced fresh parsley
1 tablespoon minced fresh chives

Garnish:
2 tablespoons grated Parmesan
    cheese (more if individual baking
    dishes are used)
Parsley sprigs

Peel and devein shrimp, leaving last joint and tail on. Butterfly by slitting shrimp along vein cavity without cutting through. Gently spread shrimp open and place in bowl. Pour cream over and refrigerate for 30 minutes, stirring occasionally.

Meanwhile, prepare sauce: Whisk lemon juice, egg yolk, pepper, salt and garlic together in a small, heavy saucepan. Add 4 tablespoons of chilled butter, cut into bits. Place over medium-low heat and stir until butter is melted. Add remaining 4 tablespoons of chilled butter, cut into bits, and whisk briskly over medium-low heat until butter is incorporated and slightly thickened. Remove from heat and stir in parsley and chives. Set aside until needed.

Drain shrimp and discard cream. Dredge shrimp in flour. In a large skillet over medium high heat, heat oil. Arrange shrimp, open side down, and sauté for 5 minutes. Do not turn shrimp. Remove shrimp, drain briefly, then arrange in baking dish.

Place under preheated broiler and broil 5 minutes or until golden. Pour sauce over shrimp, sprinkle with grated Parmesan cheese and run under broiler briefly to melt cheese.

Garnish with fresh parsley sprigs. Serves 4 as an entrée. Serve with lightly buttered angel hair pasta, a green salad and garlic bread to mop up the sauce.

To serve 8 as an appetizer: arrange shrimp in 8 smaller baking dishes. Continue with recipe, dividing sauce among the dishes. Serve with garlic bread slices. Medium-size shrimp is recommended for smaller servings.

67

Carol Nahinu's Onolicious Fish recipe comes all the way from Japan.

Because of the abundant supply of fresh fish in Hawaii and the demand for ethnic foods, **Carol Nahinu's Onolicious Fish** has become a party hit.

Nahinu's father, a retired school principal, was the cook of the family and greatly influenced Nahinu. But cooking became serious business for Nahinu only after marriage. A working wife and mother of a four-year-old daughter, Nahinu likes to concoct her own specialties. She prefers fresh food and she prepares everything herself.

Nahinu says that about 20 years ago her mother took a cooking class while visiting with relatives in Japan. She was looking for a good fish recipe, found it and shared it with Nahinu.

68

Onolicious Fish

1 pound fish fillet (mahi-mahi, aku,
    ahi or au)
1 egg
1-1/2 teaspoons curry powder
1 teaspoon salt
1 tablespoon sake (brandy or
    whiskey can be substituted)
1 tablespoon shoyu
1 tablespoon sugar
1 tablespoon flour
2 teaspoons cornstarch

Slash fish in diagonals (do not cut through fish) for easy soaking. Beat egg, curry powder, salt, sake or liquor, shoyu and sugar. Soak fish in this sauce and mix well. Let stand for 30 to 60 minutes. Remove fish and sprinkle with a mixture of flour and cornstarch and deep-fry slowly over moderate heat.

Judy Stucke with her Nut-Crusted Sole.

As a high school student in Massachusetts, **Judy Stucke** won top honors in a Betty Crocker homemaking contest, even though she was a tomboy and never cooked. She said she never creates her own dishes but whenever she finds a great recipe, she clips it and puts it in her files. She uses her microwave oven whenever possible.

Stucke, a registered nurse at Queen's Medical Center and the mother of two young children, found the recipe for **Nut-Crusted Sole** in a magazine about five years ago. She clipped the recipe because she's always looking for different ways to prepare fish. It's easy to prepare, and even people who don't like fish seem to enjoy it. She especially likes the almonds.

Nut-Crusted Sole

1 pound sole
1/3 cup finely chopped almonds
3 tablespoons wheat germ
1/4 teaspoon salt
1/8 teaspon paprika
2 tablespoons sour cream
2 tablespoons mayonnaise
1 teaspoon lemon juice
1/2 teaspoon soy sauce
Dash onion powder

Combine almonds, wheat germ, salt and paprika. In a small bowl, stir together sour cream, mayonnaise, lemon juice, soy sauce and onion powder. Arrange fish on greased aluminum foil in a shallow baking pan or cookie sheet. Spread with mayonnaise mixture and then top with nut mixture. Bake at 400 degrees for about 20 minutes or until fish flakes easily. Makes 4 servings.

To reduce fat content, substitute yogurt for the sour cream.

Steven Tseu's salmon baked in foil is easy to prepare, versatile and flavorful.

Steven Tseu enjoys Chinese food, but prefers to cook intercontinental dishes. He and his wife, Geri, like to experiment with recipes on weekends. She prepares mostly American dishes such as fried chicken and roast meat, but he's more adventuresome.

Tseu, a brokerage manager, said of **Salmon Confetti:** "While attending college in Washington state I often went to the Sound to fish for fresh salmon. Since the salmon was so abundant, I always returned home with at least one fish for dinner. After I had spent months preparing salmon in just about every way possible, a friend of mine introduced me to this terrific salmon dish."

72

Salmon Confetti

1 (3- to 4-pound) salmon, butterflied
    (salmon steaks may be used in
    place of a whole fish)
1-1/2 cups mayonnaise (can use
    light or low-cholesterol)
1 large Maui onion, diced
2 large tomatoes, diced
1/2 pound fresh mushrooms, diced
1/2 package (1/2 cup) smoked
    bacon, diced
2 tablespoons capers
Juice from 1/2 lemon
Salt and pepper to taste

Dice 1/2 package of bacon in pan and brown 3 to 4 minutes on medium-high heat.

Rinse the salmon and pat dry. Place the butterflied salmon skin-side down. Spread mayonnaise evenly over the entire salmon. Place the diced onion, tomato, mushroom and bacon on the fish. Then spoon the capers over the filling. Squeeze juice from 1/2 lemon over the entire fish. You may want to use less juice since capers also are added. Finally, sprinkle some salt and pepper over the fish and stuffing.

Cover the salmon tightly with foil and place it in a 425-degree oven and bake for about 35 to 45 minutes, or until the vegetables are slightly cooked and the fish is tender.

When the fish is done, it will look as if a handful of confetti was thrown on top of it.

The fish goes well with rice, mashed potatoes, or freshly baked French bread. Either white wine or beer will complement this dish nicely.

Carol Banks submitted Mom's Korean Somen with Zucchini so others could enjoy it too.

This recipe originated in Korea, where an expectant mother had a craving for zucchini. Because she liked this vegetable so much, she mixed and matched it with other ingredients and came up with a winner: **Mom's Korean Somen with Zucchini**.

Carol Banks, who is with *This Week* Magazine in Honolulu, was adopted when her Korean mother married Walter Banks while he was serving with the U. S. Army in Korea during the 1960s.

A soon-to-be-bride, Banks learned the basics from her mother, but likes to re-do her mom's recipes to suit her style.

Banks said she likes her dishes hot and dumps all kinds of ingredients in her recipes. Her mom advises her to keep it simple, but she has praised Banks often for her spaghetti dishes.

Mom's Korean Somen With Zucchini

1 large zucchini (or 2 small ones), cut into 1/4-inch slices, then julienned into 1/8-inch strips
1/2 large onion, sliced
1/2 pound somen noodles, or other type of thin noodles
3 tablespoons butter or margarine
Dash of MSG
1 tablespoon garlic powder
Salt and pepper to taste
Red pepper flakes to taste
Dash of vinegar

Sauce:
1/2 cup soy sauce
2 tablespoons sesame oil

Put somen into a pot of boiling water and cook until done, about 10 to 12 minutes or less. Keep checking. Drain noodles and leave in refrigerator while making the zucchini in its sauce.

For the sauce, heat skillet on medium heat. Melt butter; then add julienned strips of zucchini and sliced onion and stir. Add salt, pepper, garlic powder, red pepper flakes, MSG, and vinegar to zucchini. Continue to stir until the zucchini is almost cooked. Then add soy sauce and sesame oil. Stir until fully cooked.

Then add the cold noodles to the zucchini and sauce in the skillet. Stir together until thoroughly mixed. Cover the whole mixture in a large bowl with plastic wrap and refrigerate. Leave in refrigerator for 30 minutes, or until completely cold. Take bowl out of the refrigerator and serve cold.

You can top noodles with kamaboko (fishcake) slices, nori (dried seaweed) and fried eggs sliced julienne-style.

Advertiser **photo by T. Umeda**
Keiko Kai's platter of Fried Soba is made from buckwheat.

You can't change the environment, but you can change what you eat, according to **Keiko Kai**, whose **Fried Soba** is rich in vitamins and minerals. Originally from Tokyo, Kai is a food consultant specializing in macrobiotic cooking, which is similar to vegetarian cooking, but emphasizes whole grain products. She also speaks to groups and writes in her spare time.

Kai and her husband, Mutsuoki, a psychiatrist, met in Japan 19 years ago and were married before moving to the U.S. East Coast, where he had a practice. They came to Hawaii 10 years ago and have two children, ages 9 and 7.

76

Fried Soba

2 packages soba (cook according to
   package directions)
1 carrot, coarsely shredded
Bok choy or cabbage, chopped in
   1/4- to 1/2-inch lengths
2 leeks or one bunch of green onion
2 to 3 shiitake mushrooms
1 package bean sprouts
2 tablespoons kuzu, arrowroot or
   cornstarch
1/2 green pepper, chopped well
1 clove garlic, minced or pressed
1-inch piece ginger, grated
Sesame oil
2 tablespoons tamari or shoyu
2 to 3 tablespoons Worcestershire
   sauce to taste
Black pepper and salt to taste

*This simple-to-make, healthful dish
is perfect for potluck parties.*

Boil soba, rinse well with water and
drain. Soak mushrooms in 2 cups of
lukewarm water for 20 to 30
minutes; then cut off stems and
discard. Slice the rest of mushrooms in strips and save the water.

   Fry ginger and garlic in frying
pan coated with small amount of
sesame oil.

   Fry vegetables in the following
order: carrots, green pepper, bok
choy, mushrooms, bean sprouts
and green onion.

   Mix kuzu into the water saved
after soaking the mushrooms. Pour
into the pan and mix. Add shoyu or
tamari and Worcestershire sauces.

   Fry soba in a separate pan and
season with salt and pepper. Place
soba on a large plate and put fried
vegetables on the top.

Advertiser **photo by Richard Ambo**

Shirley Maeshiro's Spinach-Mushroom Casserole can be served as an entrée or as a side dish.

As a working wife and mother of two young children, **Shirley Maeshiro** has learned to rely on quick meals. **Spinach-Mushroom Casserole** is a favorite because it is simple to make, inexpensive, and delicious. It can be made a day ahead and refrigerated, then reheated the next day or served cold.

Maeshiro obtained the recipe from a friend at a dinner party. She likes to serve it with a chilled salad and warm bread. Her guests think she spent all day in the kitchen!

A claims adjustor for Island Insurance Company and a home economics major, Maeshiro loves to eat but hates to cook, so she's always on the lookout for quick and easy dishes. She prefers Island-style food, such as stir-fry, which doesn't really require a recipe.

Spinach-Mushroom Casserole

2 (10-ounce) packages frozen
    spinach
3 tablespoons butter
1 small onion, diced
1/4 pound fresh mushrooms,
    chopped
4 eggs
1/4 cup fine bread crumbs
1 can condensed cream of
    mushroom soup
1/4 cup Parmesan cheese
1/8 teaspoon pepper
1/8 teaspoon basil
1/8 teaspoon oregano

Place spinach under hot water to thaw. Strain water out thoroughly. Set aside. Melt butter and fry onions and mushrooms. Stir in cream of mushroom soup, add beaten eggs with bread crumbs, mix in spices and fold in spinach. Place mixture in a 9- by 9-inch pan or Pyrex® bowl. Top with Parmesan cheese. Bake at 325 degrees for 30 minutes. Serve warm or chilled.

Marsha Meckler's Quick Quiche is a good way to use ingredients at your fingertips.

Soon after her arrival from Cleveland, Ohio, **Marsha Meckler** went grocery shopping and got "sticker shock." She was flabbergasted at the high cost of food and immediately started looking for bargains. Her **Quick Quiche** recipe is an economical dish that allows you to use ingredients you have on hand.

Meckler, a legal-writing consultant, is extremely well organized and has alphabetized more than 2,000 recipes in numbered envelopes. They're stored in shoe boxes for easy access. She also makes good use of her cookbooks, incorporating recipes to suit her taste.

Meckler's husband, Michael Weinstein, is an associate professor of sociology at the University of Hawaii.

Quick Quiche

Crust layer:
3 eggs
1-1/2 cups milk
1/2 stick (4 tablespoons) melted
    margarine (optional)
1/4 teaspoon salt (optional)
1/2 cup Bisquick®

Filling:
2 cups shredded cheese (any variety
    or combination of 2; can use
    light cheese)
2 to 3 cups meats, vegetables, or
    combinations, cut in bite-sized
    pieces
1/4 cup chopped onion (yellow or
    red or scallions)
1/2 teaspoon basil
1/2 teaspoon oregano

*Quick Quiche is wonderful to serve
when you haven't planned ahead
for dinner. You can use just about
anything in it, as long as you like
the combination of flavors.*

Blend together, by hand or with mixer, the crust ingredients. Mixture may be a little lumpy. Pour into a greased 9- by 13-inch pan. Sprinkle cheese on top of the crust. Do not stir into the crust.

Add vegetables (mushrooms, frozen or fresh chopped broccoli, green pepper, zucchini), or meats (small pieces of cooked bacon, leftover ham or chicken) or both. Add onion. Sprinkle with basil and oregano. Add other herbs and spices you like, such as dill weed, garlic or garlic powder, black pepper, or marjoram.

Bake at 350 degrees (325 for Pyrex® pan) for 40 to 50 minutes, or until crust browns and knife inserted into mixture is not wet.

Shirley Souza's Cold Vegetable Pizza is perfect for potlucks.

Shirley Souza obtained the recipe for **Cold Vegetable Pizza** from a cousin in California. Colorful, delicious, easy and cool, the dish is perfect for Hawaii's warm climate. Souza likes to take the pizza to potlucks, and always gets lots of requests for the recipe.

A former housekeeper with Liberty House, Souza is retired and lives with her son, daughter-in-law and two grandchildren. Her teen-age granddaughter loves the pizza so much she eats it for breakfast!

Souza doesn't care much for cooking, so she uses the crock pot a lot and likes to stir-fry.

Cold Vegetable Pizza

Crust:
2 packages crescent rolls

Spread:
2 (8-ounce) tubs of soft cream
    cheese (can use light)
1 cup mayonnaise
1 package original ranch dressing

Vegetables:
1 bunch broccoli, bite-size pieces
1 bunch cauliflower
6 fresh mushrooms
1 bell pepper (optional)
1 medium-size can black olives
1 large or 2 medium-size carrots,
    grated

Topping:
Shredded cheddar or mozzarella
    cheese or both

Roll out crescent rolls on greased
11- by 16-inch shallow cookie sheet,
spreading dough out with edges up.
Bake at 375 degrees for 10 minutes.
Let cool.

With electric mixer, combine
cream cheese, mayonnaise and
ranch dressing. Spread mixture on
crust. Arrange vegetables on
mixture, sprinkling grated carrots
on last. Then sprinkle on desired
amount of cheese. Press down
ingredients, cover with foil and
refrigerate. Slice before serving.

Advertiser photo by T. Umeda

Nancy Stenstrom's Eggplant Parmesan takes time to prepare, but is worth it.

Nancy Stenstrom's mother taught her the basics, but Stenstrom claims she always had a knack for cooking, coming from a family of talented cooks. The **Eggplant Parmesan** is a family recipe that was handed down from one generation to another. She obtained the sauce recipe from her Italian Aunt Marie.

Stenstrom, a mother of two children, is a flight attendant with United Air Lines three times a week. Because of her hectic schedule, she has a live-in nanny to take care of the children. But Stenstrom does all the cooking--freezing casseroles and lasagna sections so they can be reheated while she's gone. She leans toward vegetarian dishes because she's concerned about her family's health. Her husband, Tom, and her children love this dish.

Eggplant Parmesan

2 large eggplant, unpeeled and
       sliced 1/4-inch thick
1 (8-ounce) can Parmesan cheese
1 (6-ounce) can tomato paste
1 (15-ounce) can tomato sauce
1/2 teaspoon oregano
1/4 cup parsley flakes
1 large onion, chopped
1 clove garlic, minced
2 tablespoons maple syrup
4 eggs
2 cups cracker crumbs
1/2 cup vegetable oil
1 cup milk
2 cups shredded mozzarella cheese

For sauce: In cooking pot, add 1 large can tomato sauce, tomato paste, oregano, parsley flakes, onion, garlic and maple syrup. Bring to boil; simmer 30 minutes.

For eggplant: Scramble eggs and milk in large bowl. Dip eggplant slices into mixture. Fill separate bowl with cracker crumbs and dip eggplant. Heat oil in frying pan. Fry eggplant slices until tender. Dry on paper towel to soak up excess oil.

In baking pan, place 1 layer of fried eggplant (6 slices), topped by sauce, mozzarella and Parmesan cheeses. Repeat until there are 3 layers. Top with leftover tomato sauce and cheeses. Preheat oven to 350 degrees. Bake for 30 minutes. Serve with crisp green salad. Serves 6.

Double the recipe and freeze leftovers for an effort-free second meal.

Desserts

Dorothy Amoral discovered her Mochi Mango Bread by accident.

Her neighbors provided the mangoes, so **Dorothy Amoral** baked the bread. This give-and-take deal went on for years until one day Amoral ran out of flour while putting together the ingredients.

It was too late to rush to the market, so she looked through the cupboard for a substitute and found mochiko flour (rice flour). Amoral used that in place of the wheat flour and added Bisquick®. According to Amoral, the **Mochi Mango Bread** turned out better than the original one, because it's moist, almost like a pudding, and has mochi-like consistency.

Amoral, a postal clerk at Holiday Mart, was born on Maui, has lived in the Islands all her life, and has 9 grandchildren. She insists she cooks only out of necessity, but her husband, Richard, thinks she's a pretty good cook.

Mochi Mango Bread

3 cups mochiko flour
1 cup Bisquick®
4 teaspoons baking soda
4 teaspoons pumpkin pie spice
1 teaspoon salt
3 cups sugar
1-1/2 cups salad oil
2 teaspoons vanilla
6 eggs, unbeaten
8 cups diced mango (ripe and firm)
1 cup raisins
1 cup flaked coconut
1 cup chopped walnuts or
    macadamia nuts

Mix together mochiko flour, Bisquick®, baking soda, pumpkin pie spice, salt and sugar. Mix oil and vanilla together and add to the dry ingredients; then add unbeaten eggs. Mix well until the ingredients are blended. Add diced mango and mix lightly to coat. Add raisins, flaked coconut and walnuts or macadamia nuts. Let sit for 5 to 10 minutes before putting in the oven.

Makes 4 large loaves (8-1/2- by 4-1/2-inch aluminum foil pans) or 9 small loaves (7- by 3-1/2-inch aluminum foil pans). Pour mixture into greased pans and bake at 350 degrees. For large loaves, bake 1 hour, and for small loaves, 45 minutes. Optional: Pour 1 tablespoon brandy over each loaf before serving. The bread freezes well and makes a nice gift.

Advertiser **photo by Charles Okamura**

Robin Benedict's Sensational and Simple Mango Dream Cake is just a piece of cake to make.

Robin Benedict enjoys baking so much that she enrolled in a cake-decorating class a couple of years ago. Since then she has baked two wedding cakes and many birthday and shower cakes.

She learned basic cooking from her grandmother. Benedict's mother died when she was very young, so she lived with her grandmother, two cousins and an aunt. Her grandmother cooked lots of Portuguese dishes, but would only let the children stir the food in the pot. As they grew older, Benedict and her cousins were allowed to help their grandmother with the cooking.

Benedict, mother of two children and a clerk at the State of Hawaii Department of Human Services, created **Sensational and Simple Mango Dream Cake** for mothers who never seem to have much time, but who want something special.

Sensational and Simple Mango Dream Cake

1 box yellow cake mix
1/2 cup oil
4 eggs
1 cup ripe mango (or banana) purée
1/2 cup water

Topping:
1 (8-ounce) container Cool Whip®
1/3 cup milk
1 (3-1/2-ounce) box instant vanilla
    pudding
1 cup ripe mango (or banana) purée

For cake, combine all the ingredients and pour into a 9- by 13-inch pan. Bake at 350 degrees for about 30 minutes until the cake is done.

For topping: Combine all the ingredients and set in refrigerator until the cake is cooled. Do not remove the cake from the pan.

Pour topping on cooled cake and return to refrigerator for 1 hour before serving for best results.

If you don't have mangoes,
substitute bananas.

Carolyn Carvalho's Fluffy Banana Bread draws raves from everyone.

There was a time when **Carolyn Carvalho** couldn't even put together a decent bowl of saimin. She says she could barely boil water. But when she got married she had to learn fast. Today Carvalho loves to cook and experiment whenever she has the time, and the **Fluffy Banana Bread** is her husband's favorite dessert.

Carvalho, a part-time student and the mother of a 4-year-old boy, is not sure where she acquired the recipe, but thinks it may have appeared on a calendar about nine years ago. The original recipe has been modified over the years to make it lighter and fluffier. She said the trick is to add the dry ingredients a little at a time.

Fluffy Banana Bread

1/2 cup butter
1 cup sugar
2 eggs
1 teaspoon vanilla
1-2/3 cups flour
1 teaspoon baking soda
1/2 teaspoon salt
1 cup mashed bananas
1/2 cup sour cream
1/2 cup chopped nuts

In a large bowl cream butter, sugar and vanilla well. Add eggs one at a time and beat well until fluffy.

Sift dry ingredients and add them alternately with the bananas and sour cream to the butter mixture, small amounts at a time. End with the dry ingredients and mix gently. Add nuts. Bake at 350 degrees for 1 hour.

My Mother's Turkish Friend's Cake is Love Dean's favorite dessert.

My Mother's Turkish Friend's Cake was a special delight whenever **Love Dean**'s mother baked it back in New York City. Her mother liked the recipe because it was quick and easy, yet tasted exotic. Dean liked the cake and its name, which she thought was "Turkissfrens."

Dean treasures the recipe because it was passed down to her by her mother, and it brings back fond memories. Dean, in turn, made the cake often for her daughter, Karen, when she was growing up.

Dean, who writes history books on lighthouses, enjoys cooking, but sticks to light, simple and healthful dishes such as stir-frys done Oriental style.

My Mother's Turkish Friend's Cake

1 cup brown sugar
2 cups sifted whole wheat flour
2 tablespoons instant coffee
1/2 teaspoon cinnamon
2 teaspoons nutmeg
1/2 cup butter or margarine
1 cup sour cream or yogurt
1 beaten egg
1 teaspoon baking soda
1/2 cup chopped nuts

In a bowl, mix together sugar, flour, instant coffee, cinnamon and nutmeg. Cut butter or margarine into the mixture. Put about half the mixture on the bottom of an 8- by 8-inch pan and press evenly. To the remaining mixture in the bowl, add sour cream or yogurt, beaten egg, baking soda and chopped nuts (your preference). Stir until well blended. Place mixture over the bottom layer and bake about 20 to 30 minutes at 350 degrees.

Advertiser photo by Charles Okamura

Melissa Gionet's Tucson Lemon Cake is light and lemony, with the special flavor of poppy seeds.

The **Tucson Lemon Cake** submitted by **Melissa Gionet** is dramatically shot through with poppy seeds, which give it a flavor all its own. It's further enhanced by the lemon glaze, which soaks through the cake while it's still hot.

Gionet, who is with the law firm of Case & Lynch, has been in Hawaii less than a year. Originally from New York, she learned to cook from her father, who is especially good at preparing Chinese and Thai dishes. Her mother likes to bake.

Gionet received this recipe from a friend. It was on the back of the recipe the friend was recommending, but it sounded so good she tried it instead.

96

Tucson Lemon Cake

1-1/2 cups sugar
1/2 cup margarine or butter,
    softened
3 eggs
2-1/2 cups all-purpose flour
1 teaspoon baking soda
1/2 teaspoon salt
1 cup buttermilk
1/4 cup poppy seeds
2 tablespoons grated lemon peel
2 tablespoons lemon juice

Lemon Glaze:
Mix together
2 cups powdered sugar
1/4 cup margarine or butter, melted
2 tablespoons grated lemon peel
1/4 cup lemon juice

Heat oven to 325 degrees. Grease
and flour 12-cup Bundt cake pan or
10- by 4-inch tube pan. Beat sugar
and margarine in large bowl on
medium speed until light and fluffy.
Beat in eggs, 1 at a time.

Mix flour, baking soda and salt;
beat into sugar mixture alternately
with buttermilk until well blended.
Stir in poppy seed, lemon peel and
lemon juice. Spread in pan.

Bake until wooden pick inserted
in center comes out clean, 50 to 55
minutes. Immediately poke holes in
top of cake with long-tined fork;
pour about 2/3 of the Lemon Glaze
over top.

Cool 20 minutes. Invert on heat-
proof serving plate; remove pan.
Spread with remaining glaze. Makes
16 servings.

Jennie Goya's Red Bean Shortbread Delight is her own creation.

By adding red beans between layers, **Jennie Goya** has turned an ordinary shortbread into a yummy dessert. **Red Bean Shortbread Delight** tastes a little like Japanese manju but is flakier and tastier.

Goya, a secretary at Hickam Air Force Base, obtained the shortbread recipe from a friend who's a good baker. But the bean filling was her own concoction. You can even make the filling with Okinawan sweet potatoes, the purple version. Boil the potatoes first and then mash them before placing on the bottom layer.

Goya thought she'd share the recipe with *Advertiser* readers because whenever she takes the shortbread to gatherings, everyone raves about it and asks for the recipe.

Red Bean Shortbread Delight

1 pound butter
1 cup sugar
4-1/2 cups flour
1 tablespoon vanilla
1 large can Tsubushian (red bean mixture)

Cream butter and sugar together. Add vanilla and stir. Then add flour and mix to form a dough. Place half of dough in a rectangular (about 10-by 14-inch) baking pan. Spread dough to cover bottom of the pan. Then spread red bean mixture over the dough. Top with remaining dough. Bake for 45 minutes in a 375-degree oven.

Note: Here's a little tip from Goya. If you have problems pressing the top dough onto the bean mixture, flatten it first, then press down dough a little at a time, pinching it as you go along.

Advertiser **photo by T. Umeda**
Doris Iwano's San Quentin Cake is easy to make.

Doris Iwano says that the recipe for **San Quentin Cake** actually came from within the prison walls. Iwano got the recipe from a friend, who got it from a former prison employee.

The recipe is Iwano's favorite because it's popular with family and friends, tastes good warm or cold, can be frozen, and because apples, the main ingredient, are available all year round. It tastes like apple pie, but has the texture of a cake. Those who prefer a richer cake can top it with vanilla pudding.

San Quentin Cake

2 cups chopped apples (can use
    green baking apples)
1 egg
1 cup sugar
1/2 cup oil (any type of vegetable oil)
1 cup flour
1/2 teaspoon baking soda
1/2 teaspoon salt
1 teaspoon cinnamon
1/2 cup raisins

Place ingredients in a bowl in order
given. Mix just enough to blend;
then pour into an 8- by 8-inch pan
lined with wax paper. Smooth out
wax paper so there won't be creases
in the corners. There's no need to
grease. The cake also can be baked
directly in the pan, but grease first
and sprinkle with flour.

Bake at 350 degrees for 1 hour.

Advertiser **photo by Charles Okamura**

Cheri Keefer's Black Bottom Cups are a blue-ribbon winner in her book.

Cheri Keefer says she'd rather have a piece of cake and sacrifice some other food. She has a sweet tooth and so does her husband, Bob.

Keefer teaches art at Iolani School and is one of the track team coaches. She grew up on a farm, where her father raised cattle and wheat. Being the only child, she helped her mother prepare meals for the hired hands. While in high school she won the Betty Crocker Homemaking Award for her essay on cooking and sewing.

Keefer said this recipe was hard to turn down when a friend shared it with her at a party. She ate four **Black Bottom Cups** before she realized it. Keefer's friend works out with her at the Honolulu Club and they are always talking about easy but outstanding recipes.

Black Bottom Cups

1 (8-ounce) package cream cheese,
    softened
1 egg
1/3 cup sugar
1/8 teaspoon salt
3/4 package (12 ounces) semi-sweet
    chocolate morsels (nuts can be
    added)
1-1/2 cups flour
1 cup sugar
1/4 cup unsweetened cocoa
1 teaspoon soda
1/2 teaspoon salt
1 cup water
1/3 cup oil
1 tablespoon vinegar
1 teaspoon vanilla

Combine in a mixing bowl cream
cheese, egg, 1/3 cup sugar and 1/8
teaspoon salt. Beat well. Then stir
in chocolate morsels and nuts
(optional).

Sift together flour, 1 cup sugar,
unsweetened cocoa, soda and 1/2
teaspoon salt. Add to the cream
cheese, chocolate morsels and nut
mixture with water, oil, vinegar and
vanilla. Beat until well combined.
Mixture will be quite thin. It's best
to use a measuring cup to pour into
muffin tin or cups. Fill muffin cup
half full; then top with heaping
tablespoon of cream cheese
mixture. Bake at 350 degrees for
about 25 minutes. Makes 1-1/2
dozen.

*Keefer suggests you double or triple
the recipe when you make it--
one batch goes so quickly.*

Laurel Leslie's Rainbow Layer Cake.

Laurel Leslie loves to bake because desserts are dramatic--a great finale to parties. She jokingly said that her idea of a good meal is a small entrée and a big dessert. Leslie likes to experiment with desserts because they're the most versatile. But when she bakes and leaves a dessert in the freezer, it doesn't last long.

The dessert snatchers include her husband, Albert Smith, and two grown-up children. Leslie, who spent her teen-age years in Kihei, Maui, says she has had a keen interest in activites in and around the kitchen since her earliest years. Encouraged by her nurturing mother and several caring teachers, her interest grew into a degree from San Diego State University in foods and nutrition.

Rainbow Layer Cake

4 egg yolks
1/4 cup sugar
1/2 teaspoon vanilla
1/2 teaspoon lemon extract
4 egg whites
1/2 cup sugar
3/4 cup cake flour
1 teaspoon baking powder
1/4 teaspoon salt
1 pint lime sherbet
1 pint guava sherbet

Beat egg yolks until thick and lemon colored. Gradually beat in 1/4 cup sugar, vanilla and lemon extract. With clean beaters, beat egg whites until almost stiff, gradually adding remaining 1/2 cup sugar, and beat until very stiff. Fold yolks into whites. Sift flour, baking powder and salt together. Fold into egg mixture.

Bake in greased, waxed paper-lined 15- by 10-1/2-inch jelly roll pan. Press down dough to fit the size of the pan; then bake at 350 degrees for 12 minutes. Remove cake from pan. Peel off paper carefully, trim crusts from the cake and refrigerate for 1 hour or longer.

Layering cake: It is best to work with chilled or frozen cake and pan. Cut cake to fit into an 8- by 4-inch bread or loaf pan (a metal one with straight sides is best). There should be 3 layers. Place a generous layer of lime sherbet (1/2-inch thick) on the bottom layer of cake. Then place another layer of cake on top of the sherbet. Add guava sherbet in a layer 1/2-inch thick. Place the third layer of cake on top. The top of the cake may be covered with whipping cream or a reasonable substitute. Freeze until firm.

To serve, slice cake 1-1/2 inches thick and garnish with mint. Serves 8.

Note: A pound cake from the market may be substituted for the jelly roll, but you may end up with a heavier dessert.

Advertiser **photo by Charles Okamura**

Kristen McHargue's Piña Colada Cake is light and delicious--just right for Hawaii's warm climate.

When **Kristen McHargue** got married three years ago, her mother presented her with a box full of priceless family recipes as a wedding gift. In it was a dessert recipe, **Piña Colada Cake**, which McHargue used to enjoy back home in Nebraska.

McHargue and her husband, Steve, came to the Islands in December, 1990, when both acquired jobs with a Honolulu

family. She does household management and he takes care of the property. When the family has dinner parties, McHargue makes all the arrangements, sometimes planning the menu and cooking. She acquired her love for cooking from her mother, a gourmet chef, who teaches cooking in Nebraska.

Piña Colada Cake

1 box white cake mix (without
    pudding)
1 (8-ounce) can cream of coconut
    (supermarket liquor section)
1 (16-ounce) can crushed pineapple
8 ounces whipped cram
1/4 package coconut, toasted

Bake the cake in a 9- by 13-inch
pan according to the package
directions. Remove cake from oven
and immediately punch holes in it
with the handle of a wooden spoon.
While the cake is hot, pour the
cream of coconut over the entire
surface. Spoon a layer of crushed
pineapple over the cake. Cool the
cake.

Spread the whipped cream over
the cake and garnish with toasted
coconut and put in the refrigerator.
This dessert is best when made 24
hours in advance.

Advertiser photo by T. Umeda

Kathy Shirakawa's Double Chocolate Cookies have a brownie-like texture.

It took **Kathy Shirakawa** a couple of years to perfect her **Double Chocolate Cookies**. Her husband, Kazuo, enjoyed the Walnut Fudge cookies at a local cookie store so much that she decided to try to duplicate them. Now he likes her creation better than the store-bought ones.

The cookie is simple to make, but delicious, with an intense chocolate flavor and a brownie-like texture. Shirakawa thinks the instant coffee gives it a special flavor.

A former preschool teacher, Shirakawa is currently a full-time mom taking care of two young daughters. She likes to experiment when cooking, especially with pupus and entreés.

Double Chocolate Cookies

5 ounces unsweetened chocolate
1-1/3 cups sugar
1/2 cup (1 stick) butter or
    margarine, softened
2 eggs
1 tablespoon instant coffee granules
1 tablespoon vanilla extract
1 cup all-purpose flour
1/4 teaspoon salt
2 cups semi-sweet chocolate chips
1 cup coarsely chopped nuts
    (optional)

Preheat oven to 350 degrees. Lightly grease 2 cookie sheets.

Melt unsweetened chocolate over double boiler. (To microwave, place chocolate in microwave-proof bowl and heat at medium power for 1-1/2 to 4 minutes. Remove from oven and stir until smooth). Set aside melted chocolate.

Cream butter and sugar in large bowl. Add eggs one at a time, beating well after each addition. Add coffee and vanilla and blend until fluffy. Stir in melted, cooled unsweetened chocolate. Add flour and salt, mixing just until combined. Add chocolate chips and optional nuts (do not overmix). Dough will be soft.

Mound dough by 1/4 cupfuls onto prepared sheets, spacing 2 inches apart. Bake until cookies are dry in appearance and centers are still slightly soft to touch, about 15 minutes. Cool on cookie sheets 5 minutes. Transfer to rack (or brown paper bags) and cool completely. Store in airtight container. Keeps 4 days or, in freezer, 3 weeks. Makes about 18 large cookies.

Advertiser **photo by T. Umeda**

Chiyo Smith's Brownies Supreme won top honors for desserts.

Chiyo Smith admits she is a chocoholic and so are her husband, Clifford, and their four children. Smith acquired her recipe from an Ideas Book written especially for chocolate coating wafers used in candy molding. She experimented by substituting chocolate chips for the candy wafers. Since she loves caramel and macadamia nuts, it was a natural combination.

Smith owned and operated Chocolates By You, a candy-molding supply shop, for four years. She now works in the business office at Queen's Medical Center. At Queen's she also won a prize for **Brownies Supreme**.

"My Best Recipe" contest judges were impressed with Smith's brownies, which include melted caramel and macadamia nuts, adding to the richness and moistness.

Brownies Supreme

1-1/2 cups semi-sweet chocolate
   chips
1 stick margarine or butter
1-3/4 cups sugar
4 eggs
2 cups flour
1 teaspoon baking powder
1 teaspoon salt

Center filling:
30 caramel cubes
2 tablespoons milk
5 ounces macadamia nuts, coarsely
   chopped

Icing:
1 stick margarine or butter
1/3 cup milk
3 tablespoons cocoa
1 teaspoon vanilla
1 pound powdered sugar

Preheat oven to 350 degrees. Melt chocolate and margarine together in microwave on defrost for 1 to 2 minutes; then remove. Stir in sugar and add the eggs one at a time, beating well after each addition. Stir in the flour, baking powder and salt, which have been mixed together. Spread half of the batter in a 9- by 13-inch buttered pan.

For the center filling, melt caramels and milk in microwave for 2 to 3 minutes on defrost. Spread over batter. Add half of the coarsely chopped macadamia nuts and spread over batter. Add remaining batter. Bake for 40 to 45 minutes. (Do not use toothpick to test for doneness; brownies should be moist.)

Prepare icing by melting margarine in microwave for 45 seconds on high. Add rest of the ingredients. Spread on the cake while it is hot. Sprinkle rest of the macadamia nuts, chopped to desired coarseness, on the top of the icing. Cool and cut into bars.

Note: For those who prefer to melt the caramel or margarine using the stove method, a double boiler or a pot is sufficient, but turn the heat very low because chocolate tends to melt too fast.

Lt. Col. Linda Thorpe's Oreo Cheesecake is an elegant dessert.

Lt. Col. Linda Thorpe, who has served in the Army for 21 years, has very little time for domestic chores such as baking, but when she does, she always manages to come up with a winner.

This cheesecake, according to Thorpe, is a favorite of family, friends and co-workers at Tripler Army Medical Center, where Thorpe is chief of anesthesia nursing. Formerly of Baltimore, Maryland, she is on her third tour of duty in Hawai'i. Thorpe and her husband, Gregory, live in Foster Village with their two young daughters. Their setup is unusual; she is the breadwinner and he minds the house full-time.

112

Oreo® Cheesecake

Graham Cracker Crust:
1-1/4 cups graham cracker crumbs
1/3 cup unsalted butter, melted
1/4 cup firmly packed light brown
   sugar
1 teaspoon cinnamon

Oreo® Filling:
2 pounds cream cheese (at room
   temperature)
1-1/2 cups sugar
2 tablespoons flour
4 extra-large eggs
2 large egg yolks
1/3 cup whipping cream
2 teaspoons vanilla
1-1/2 cups coarsely chopped Oreo®
   cookies
2 cups sour cream

Swiss Fudge Glaze:
1 cup whipping cream
8 ounces semi-sweet chocolate,
   chopped
1 teaspoon vanilla
5 Oreo® cookies, halved crosswise
   (optional)

Crust: Blend all ingredients in bottom of a 10-inch springform pan, then press onto bottom and sides. Refrigerate crust until firm, 30 minutes.

Oreo® filling: Preheat oven to 425 degrees. Beat cream cheese in large bowl with electric mixer on lowest speed until smooth. Beat in 1-1/4 cups sugar and flour until blended and beat in eggs and egg yolks until mixture is smooth. Stir in cream and 1 teaspoon vanilla. Pour half of batter into crust. Sprinkle with chopped Oreo®s. Pour in remaining batter, smoothing with spatula. Bake 15 minutes. Reduce oven temperature to 225 degrees. Bake 50 minutes, covering top loosely with foil if browning too quickly. Increase oven temperature to 350 degrees.

Blend sour cream, remaining 1/4 cup sugar and 1 teaspoon vanilla in small bowl. Spread over cake and bake 7 minutes. Refrigerate immediately. Cover and chill overnight.

Swiss Fudge Glaze: Scald cream in heavy medium saucepan over high heat. Add chocolate and vanilla. Stir 1 minute. Remove from heat and stir until all the chocolate is melted. Refrigerate glaze for 10 minutes.

Set cake on platter and remove springform. Pour glaze over cake. Arrange Oreo® halves, cut side down, around outer edge of cake.

With a cup of Kona coffee, this dessert is an elegant end to a meal.

113

Judy Glassmaker's Peanut-Chocolate Parfait Dessert is not for dieters.

Judy Glassmaker said her **Peanut-Chocolate Parfait Dessert** has everything wonderful and fattening in it. She found the recipe in the newspaper a number of years ago while she was living in Scottsdale, Arizona.

"My Best Recipe" judges thought the combination of peanut butter and chocolate was interesting and they commented favorably on the light cream cheese topping with the sprinkling of peanuts and grated chocolate.

Glassmaker, a wire operator with Dean Witter Reynolds Inc., won first prize for Peanut-Chocolate Parfait Dessert at her office Christmas Pupu Contest.

Peanut-Chocolate Parfait Dessert

1 (18-1/2-ounce) package pudding-
    included devil's food cake mix
1/2 cup butter or margarine, melted
1/4 cup milk
1 egg
1-1/4 cups peanuts (dry unsalted)
3/4 cup peanut butter
1-1/2 cups powdered sugar
1 (8-ounce) package cream cheese,
    softened
2-1/2 cups milk
1 (8-ounce) container frozen
    whipped topping, thawed
1 (5-1/4-ounce) package instant
    vanilla pudding and pie filling
    mix
1 (1.45-ounce) bar milk chocolate,
    chilled and grated

Grease and flour bottom only of 13-by 9-inch pan. In large bowl, combine cake mix, butter, 1/4 cup milk, egg and 3/4 cup peanuts at medium speed of electric mixer until well blended. Spread evenly into prepared pan. Bake at 350 degrees 20 to 25 minutes. Cool.

In a small bowl, combine peanut butter and powdered sugar at low speed of electric mixer until crumbly. Set aside.

In a large bowl, beat cream cheese until smooth. Add 2-1/2 cups milk, whipped topping and pudding mix. Beat 2 minutes at low speed of electric mixer until well blended.

Pour half of cream cheese mixture over cooled base. Sprinkle with half of peanut butter mixture. Repeat with remaining cream cheese and peanut butter mixtures. Sprinkle with remaining 1/2 cup peanuts. Gently press into filling. Sprinkle with grated chocolate. Cover and refrigerate or freeze until serving time. Makes 16 servings.

Advertiser **photo by Richard Ambo**

Rita Ihly's Poppy Seed Torte is a rich and sumptuous dessert.

After 37 years in Alaska's wilderness, **Rita Ihly** decided it was time for a change, so she came to Hawaii five years ago to make her home. She first arrived here in 1978 to visit her son, who was in the navy stationed aboard a nuclear submarine at Pearl Harbor. She liked the warm climate and the nice people so returned to make her home here.

In Alaska, Ihly and her husband, who were with the Federal Aviation Administration stationed at remote airfields, had food delivered by truck, boat or airplane. She learned to bake bread because it was the only way she could get fresh loaves for her family of six.

A data technician for Seafloor Surveys International Inc., Ihly goes to Alaska frequently to visit her sons and their families, who make their homes there.

116

Poppy Seed Torte

Topping-Crust:
22 graham crackers, ground to fine
    crumbs
1/2 cup butter, melted
1/2 cup sugar

Filling:
3 cups milk
4 egg yolks
3 tablespoons poppy seeds
3 tablespoons flour
3 tablespoons cornstarch
1 cup sugar
1 teaspoon vanilla
1/2 teaspoon salt (optional)

Topping:
4 egg whites
2 tablespoons sugar
1 cup crumb mixture

For topping-crust, combine cracker crumbs, melted butter and sugar. Remove 1 cup and reserve for topping. Press remaining crumbs to cover bottom and sides of 9- by 9- or 9- by 12-inch baking pan.

For filling, combine sugar, flour, cornstarch, poppy seeds and salt in a four-quart pan. Slowly add milk, stirring into a smooth mixture. Heat at low setting, stirring constantly to prevent burning, until mixture thickens. A double boiler is suggested.

Beat egg yolks in small bowl and add some of the thickened custard mixture, blending yolks and custard. Slowly add this mixture to custard in pan, stirring constantly.

Continue to heat until thickened to custard consistency (about 3 minutes). Remove from heat and add vanilla. Pour into pan over pressed crumbs.

For topping, beat egg whites until frothy; slowly add sugar, continuing to beat until whites form peaks and are of meringue consistency. Spread over custard. Sprinkle 1 cup of crumb mixture evenly over egg whites.

Brown under broiler until topping is evenly browned. Watch this carefully so as not to burn topping.

Gail Miyashiro's Pumpkin-Apple Pie is her favorite.

It's not easy for a single parent to hold down a full-time job and care for two boys, ages 10 and 13, but **Gail Miyashiro** seems to do both effectively.

Miyashiro, who is with the City and County Building Department, said she has taught her sons the joy of baking too. She bought children's baking utensils for them and lets them do their own thing in the kitchen. At a school bake-off, the entire family walked off with prizes. Miyashiro also has won several other prizes.

Miyashiro said she found this recipe in a calendar several years ago and tried it because it combined two of her favorite pie fillings. She has modified it to make it easier and faster. The crust recipe is her mother's. This dessert has become a family favorite and a great alternative at Thanksgiving.

118

Pumpkin-Apple Pie

2 green baking apples, peeled, cored
    and sliced about 1/4-inch thick
1 lemon
1/2 teaspoon cinnamon

Filling:
1 (1-pound) can pumpkin
2 eggs, slightly beaten
1/2 cup white sugar
1/4 cup brown sugar
1 teaspoon salt
1 teaspoon cinnamon
1/2 teaspoon ginger, ground
1/4 teaspoon cloves, ground
1 (12-ounce) can evaporated milk

Crust:
3 cups flour
1 cup shortening
1 teaspoon salt
About 6 tablespoons ice water

In a bowl, toss apples with lemon juice and cinnamon. In another bowl, combine all filling ingredients in order given.

For crust, combine flour and salt. Cut in shortening until coarse crumbs are formed. Add water 1 tablespoon at a time and mix with fork until easily gathered into a ball. Divide dough in half and form into flat disk shapes. Wrap well and refrigerate for about 1 hour, then take half the dough out and form into a pastry shell. There is enough dough to make 2 deep dish (9-inch) crusts. Wrap unused dough well and freeze for later use.

Bake unpricked shell for 5 minutes in 450-degree oven. Remove and lower temperature to 375 degrees. Then arrange apples in bottom of shell. Pour filling over apples and return to oven for 1 hour or until pie tests done when knife inserted in middle comes out clean.

Carol Ann Rosenberg's Clara's Butter Horns are addicting.

According to **Carol Ann Rosenberg,** tiny pastries are very popular in New York, but you don't see them around here. Rosenberg's mother, Clara, who lives in New York, gave her the recipe. It always gets rave reviews.

Rosenberg, who moved to Hawaii four years ago from Orinda, California, is merchandise manager at Navy Exchange. She loves Italian food and Asian dishes, but hasn't learned to cook the latter yet.

Clara's Butter Horns

1 cup butter or margarine
2 cups unsifted flour, spooned into
    cup
1 egg yolk
3/4 cup sour cream
3/4 cup raisins
3/4 cup sugar
2 teaspoons cinnamon
1/2 cup nuts, chopped
1 egg white, beaten lightly

Cut butter into flour; blend in egg yolk and sour cream. Knead enough to shape into a ball.

Wrap in waxed paper; chill two hours or until firm. Cut dough into 3 equal parts; roll each of the 3 portions into a circle 1/8-inch thick on a floured board. Cut each circle into 12 triangles (as if cutting a pie).

In the meantime, blend together raisins, sugar, cinnamon and nuts; sprinkle mixture in the center of each triangle. Roll each triangle to form a crescent.

Place on ungreased cookie sheet; brush each with egg white. Bake at 375 degrees for 25 minutes or until golden brown. Makes 3 dozen.

Advertiser **photo by Carl Viti**

Jeanne Sasaki's Chocolate Icebox Pudding is a cool and chocolaty favorite.

Jeanne Sasaki loves to bake because she enjoys sweets, but to keep in shape she walks a lot and does aerobics. Her husband, Curtis, also enjoys desserts, especially chocolate.

Sasaki submitted the recipe for **Chocolate Icebox Pudding** because it is different from most recipes and allows the cook to be creative. Although the recipe calls for chocolate curls as garnish, she uses miniature chocolate morsels and sliced almonds because she had them on hand the first time she made the dessert and everyone seemed to like it that way. It's also the kind of dessert that looks as if it took all day to make (it only takes about an hour), and doesn't require turning on the oven--something we all can appreciate in Hawaii, especially in summer.

122

Chocolate Icebox Pudding

32 large or 4 cups miniature
    marshmallows
3/4 cup hot water
1/3 cup cocoa
2 tablespoons butter or margarine
1-1/2 teaspoons instant coffee
Dash of salt
1 cup chilled whipping cream
1 teaspoon vanilla
1 (3-ounce) package ladyfingers
1/2 cup chilled whipping cream
1 tablespoon sugar
1/2 teaspoon vanilla
Chocolate curls

Heat marshmallows, water, cocoa, butter, coffee and salt over medium heat, stirring constantly, until marshmallows are melted; remove from heat. Let stand until thickened, about 45 minutes.

Beat 1 cup whipping cream and 1 teaspoon vanilla in chilled small mixer bowl on high speed until stiff. Stir marshmallow mixture until blended; fold into whipped cream. Line bottom and sides of ungreased 8- by 8- by 2-inch baking dish with halved ladyfingers. Spread marshmallow mixture evenly over ladyfingers. Cover and refrigerate until set, about 5 hours.

Beat 1/2 cup whipping cream, the sugar and 1/2 teaspoon vanilla in chilled small mixer bowl on high speed until stiff. Unmold pudding on serving plate. Garnish pudding with whipped cream and chocolate curls.

Miniature chocolate morsels and sliced almonds can be used instead of chocolate curls.

Jean Schmitz's Blitz Torte is a recipe everyone requests.

Jean Schmitz, a teacher at St. Andrew's Priory, said the **Blitz Torte** was made frequently by her grandmother and mother. It is a treasured family recipe that everyone requests because it's delicious and quick to prepare.

Schmitz said she learned to cook at an early age because her father owned a dairy farm in Wisconsin. Schmitz recalls that with 12 hired hands, cooking was a major chore.

"My Best Recipe" judges expressed delight with this torte, which is not only pretty, but light in texture. Strawberries add just enough color to enhance the dessert.

Blitz Torte

1/2 cup butter
1/2 cup sugar
4 egg yolks
1 teaspoon vanilla
3 tablespoons milk
1 cup cake flour
1 teaspoon baking powder

Topping:
4 egg whites
1 cup sugar
1/2 cup almonds, sliced
Sugar and cinnamon

Sour cream filling:
1 cup sour cream
1 cup sugar
5 egg yolks, beaten
1 teaspoon almond extract
1 cup hickory nuts or pecans

Preheat oven to 350 degrees. Cream the butter and sugar. Beat egg yolks lightly and add to butter; add vanilla, milk and flour sifted with baking powder. Mix well. Spread the mixture in two greased 8-inch layer cake pans.

For topping: Beat the egg whites stiff and dry, add 1 cup of sugar gradually, and spread on the unbaked mixture in both pans. Sprinkle layers with almonds, 1 tablespoon sugar and 1/2 teaspoon cinnamon. Bake about 30 minutes. When cool, fill.

For sour cream filling: Heat cream with sugar until dissolved and pour in a steady stream on yolks, stirring constantly. Cook in a double boiler, continuing to stir until thick and smooth. Cool slightly, flavor with almond extract, and add 1 cup of hickory nuts or pecans.

Variations

Custard filling:
1 cup scalded milk
1/2 cup sugar
1 tablespoon cornstarch
2 egg yolks
1/2 teaspoon vanilla

Mix dry ingredients, add the scalded milk and pour gradually on the slightly beaten eggs. Cook in double boiler. Stir constantly until thickened; cool and flavor.

Fruit filling:
Drain well 2 (8-ounce) cans crushed pineapple and press dry with paper towel. Fold into a mixture of 1 cup whipped cream, 1-1/2 teaspoons powdered sugar and 2 teaspoons vanilla. Fill cake with the mixture and refrigerate overnight.

Note: 1 pint of fresh raspberries or strawberries may be substituted for pineapple.

Janet Shinmura's Angel Cream Pie has won numerous prizes.

Janet Shinmura's recipe for **Angel Cream Pie** has been in her files for more than 40 years and has become the star attraction at family parties, especially Thanksgiving and grandchildren's birthdays.

Shinmura acquired the recipe from a former landlady who let her taste the pie because it had just won a prize. Then Shinmura entered her own Angel Cream Pie in the Pearl City Community Fair pie contest and won first prize. One of her daughters, Donna, also was awarded top prize for the same pie while attending school.

Shinmura said she never learned to cook until she got married because her parents were such good cooks. Her father specialized in Chinese cooking and her mother in Japanese cooking.

126

Angel Cream Pie

2 teaspoons unflavored gelatin
1/2 cup sugar
2 tablespoons cornstarch
1/4 teaspoon salt
1 cup milk (can use skim milk)
3 egg yolks, slightly beaten
1-1/2 teaspoons vanilla extract
1 8-oz. bottle whipping cream,
   whipped
Milk chocolate candy, grated
1 9-inch pie shell, baked and cooled

For crust: Preheat oven to 375 degrees. Sift the flour before measuring; spoon lightly into measuring cup and level without shaking or packing down. Combine flour and salt in mixing bowl. With a pastry blender, cut shortening into the flour mixture until uniform; mixture should be fairly coarse. Sprinkle with water, a little at a time; toss with a fork. Work dough into a ball with your hands. Divide into two parts and press into flat circles with smooth edges. On a lightly floured surface, roll bottom crust to a circle about 1-1/2 inches larger than inverted pie plate. Gently ease dough into the plate. Trim edge, using trimmings to build up fluted edge. Prick with fork. Bake for 20 to 25 minutes or until golden brown. Cool.

For filling: In a double boiler, blend the gelatin, sugar, cornstarch and salt. Gradually stir in the milk. Cook over medium heat, stirring constantly until the mixture thickens and boils. Boil for 1 minute. Remove from heat. Stir the hot mixture into the egg yolks. Return the mixture to the double boiler and bring just to boiling, stirring constantly. Remove from heat and add vanilla extract.

Place the pan in a larger pan of cold water. Cool until mixture mounds slightly when dropped from a spoon. Fold in the whipping cream. Pour into cooled crust and sprinkle with grated chocolate. Refrigerate at least 6 hours or overnight. Serves 8.

_____

Shinmura always doubles the recipe because one pie is never enough.

_____

127

Laura Shipley's Apple Kuchen is delicious and easy to make.

Laura Shipley learned to cook at an early age because her father died when she was only 12 and her mother took on a job to support the family.

Originally from the state of Washington, Shipley came to Hawaii in 1977 because her husband, Ewing "Skip," was asked to manage a company. He currently owns a plumbing company and she assists whenever she has the time. Their son also helps with the business, and their married daughter lives on the East Coast.

Shipley found the recipe for **Apple Kuchen** in a women's magazine about 20 years ago. She likes it because she loves apples, it's easy to fix, and her guests always praise it.

128

Apple Kuchen

1/2 cup butter or margarine,
    softened
1 package yellow cake mix
1/2 cup flaked coconut
1 (20-ounce) can pre-sliced apples
    (pie filling apples)
1/2 cup sugar
1 teaspoon cinnamon
1 cup sour cream
1 egg

Heat oven to 350 degrees. Cut butter into cake mix; then press down and spread into a 13- by 9- by 2-inch glass pan. Bake 10 to 12 minutes. Arrange apples on warm crust, mix sugar and cinnamon together and spread over apples. Sprinkle with flaked coconut.

Mix sour cream and egg together and drizzle over top. Bake 25 to 30 minutes until edges are lightly browned; do not overbake. Serve hot with ice cream or serve cold.

Shinobu Takara shows off her Cinnamon Apple Bread Pudding.

Shinobu Takara has her own style of cooking. She may start off with someone else's recipe, but eventually revises it to suit her taste.

Formerly of Tokyo, Takara arrived here 3-1/2 years ago to attend college and stayed because she acquired a job and met Wesley, her husband, through mutual friends. Takara admits cooking is a favorite pastime because she and her husband love to eat.

Takara cooked only Japanese meals back home and says it has been an interesting experience trying out other Oriental and Western dishes.

Her husband is a typical local boy who was brought up eating American food. This forced Takara to have international variations in her recipes.

Cinnamon Apple Bread Pudding

2 cups peeled and chopped apples
2 tablespoons lemon juice
3 tablespoons cinnamon (can add
    more or less)
3 tablespoons butter
1/2 cup brown sugar
3 cups sweetbread cubes
2 cups milk
2 large eggs
1/2 cup white sugar
2 teaspoons vanilla extract
1/2 cup raisins
2 tablespoons butter, melted

Preheat oven to 350 degrees. Heat 3 tablespoons butter in a nonstick pan and sauté chopped apples and lemon juice on medium-low heat. Add brown sugar and cinnamon and continue cooking until the juice drains from the apples and thickens. Set aside.

Place bread crumbs in a 9- by 9-inch pan greased lightly with butter. Sprinkle raisins over the bread.

In a large bowl, beat eggs and add white sugar, vanilla, milk, and sautéed apple mixture. Mix well and pour over the bread cubes with raisins. Spread 2 tablespoons of melted butter over it. Bake 1 hour or until inserted knife comes out clean.

This simple, healthful, delicious dessert tastes almost like apple pie. Fresh apples enhance the flavor.

LaVonne Wicks' Double Lemon Pie in Coconut Crust is not an everyday pie.

LaVonne Wicks obtained this recipe from a California newspaper 20 to 30 years ago, and whenever she bakes it for parties, her guests love it.

A retired school teacher, Wicks and her husband, Lester, moved to Hawaii three years ago, after visiting the Islands several times. Their son and daughter and their families live on the Mainland.

Wicks experiments with different recipes, but prefers to stir-fry her food--Island style. She tries to stay within a healthful diet, but her husband loves his sweets, so she makes dessert for him once a week.

"My Best Recipe" judges were impressed with the tangy double filling, and the crust, accented with coconut, is a nice surprise.

132

Double Lemon Pie in Coconut Crust

Crust:
1 cup flour
1/3 cup butter
1/2 teaspoon salt
1/3 cup toasted coconut
2 tablespoons ice water

Filling:
1-1/4 cups sugar
4 tablespoons cornstarch
3 tablespoons flour
1/8 teaspoon salt
2 cups hot water
3 egg yolks
3 tablespoons butter
1 teaspoon grated lemon peel
1/2 cup lemon juice
1-1/2 cups whipping cream,
    whipped

For crust, sift flour and salt, cut in butter, add toasted coconut. Add water, then mix. Roll dough to fit a 9-inch pie pan. Prick the crust and bake 10 minutes in a 425-degree oven. Cool.

For filling, blend sugar, cornstarch, flour and salt with 2 cups hot water. Bring to a boil and cook slowly 15 minutes.

Beat egg yolks and add small amount to the cornstarch mixture and mix well; then add the remaining egg yolks and butter to the mixture. Cook 5 minutes more. Add lemon peel and juice. Cool.

Put 1/2 of the filling in the bottom of the crust. Then mix 1/2 of the whipped cream with remainder of filling and spread on top. Spread remainder of whipped cream on the top of the filling and sprinkle toasted coconut over it. Chill for at least 4 hours or overnight.

133

Advertiser **photo by Richard Ambo**

Martie Wright's Frosty Strawberry Squares is a light and airy dessert.

Martie Wright's favorite dessert is **Frosty Strawberry Squares** because it's fresh-tasting and pleasant, perfect when you crave something sweet, but light, after a meal.

Wright, who came to Hawaii from the Midwest 25 years ago, received the recipe from a friend about 17 years ago and has made it ever since.

She has always been interested in cooking, and taught herself how to cook. "I married at 18, so I've been cooking for a long time," she said. "Now I take care of an elderly person, so I cook for her, too. She and I have the same likes and dislikes when it comes to food, so cooking is no problem. I also like to experiment whenever I have some spare time."

Frosty Strawberry Squares

1 cup sifted flour
1/4 cup brown sugar
1/2 cup chopped walnuts
1/2 cup melted butter or margarine
2 egg whites
1 cup granulated sugar
2 cups sliced fresh strawberries
2 tablespoons lemon juice
1 cup whipping cream, whipped

Stir together first 4 ingredients; then spread evenly in shallow baking pan. Bake in 350-degree oven 20 minutes, stirring crumbs occasionally. Sprinkle 2/3 of crumbs in 13- by 9- by 2-inch pan.

Beat egg whites until they form stiff peaks, adding sugar gradually. Add berries and lemon juice and continue to whip until stiff peaks are again formed. Whip cream separately; then fold into other mixture. Spoon over crumbs; then top with remaining crumbs. Freeze 6 hours or overnight. Cut in 10 to 12 squares. Trim with whole strawberries.